THE ARTIST AND THE ACADEMY

Issues in Fine Art Education and the Wider Cultural Context

THE ARTIST AND THE ACADEMY

Issues in Fine Art Education and the
Wider Cultural Context

Edited by Nicholas de Ville and Stephen Foster

JOHN HANSARD GALLERY

THE ARTIST AND THE ACADEMY
Issues in Fine Art Education and the Wider Cultural Context
Editors: Nicholas de Ville and Stephen Foster

Published by
John Hansard Gallery
University of Southampton
Highfield
Southampton SO17 1BJ
England
Tel +44 (0) 703 592158

Printed by the University Printing Services, University of Southampton

Text based on the conference **The Artist and the Academy: European Perspectives on Today's Fine Art Education,** held at Chilworth Manor, University of Southampton on 9th and 10th December 1993; except Alexander Tzonis and Liane Lefaivre, **Why Critical Regionalism Today?** published originally in **A&U (May 1990, Volume 236, Japanese Architecture Company, Tokyo);** and Susan Hiller, **An Artist Looks at Art Education,** originally presented at the conference **The Curriculum for Fine Art in Higher Education: The Essential Elements of Fine Art courses in the '90s Tate Gallery** 19th February 1993.

Publication made possible with financial support by the Arts Council of England and the Paul Hamlyn Foundation

ISBN 0 85432 5093

Also in this series:
SPACE INVADERS: Issues of Presentation, Context and Meaning in Contemporary Art
Editors: Nicholas de Ville and Stephen Foster (1993)
ISBN 0 85432 4720

Paul Hamlyn Foundation

Acknowledgements

The editors would like to thank the authors for permission to publish their essays. Thanks are also due to the Arts Council of England and the Paul Hamlyn Foundation for financial support for this publication. We are grateful to Gerda Roper for chairing part of the original conference, and to Jill Sheridan for her work in contributing to its organisation. We should also like to thank Marl'ene Miller for transcribing many of the texts and to Libby Willis and Ros Carter for their work on the manuscript.

TABLE OF CONTENTS

I

INTRODUCTION

Nicholas de Ville and Stephen Foster

The Artist and the Academy

This publication is part of a series of debates initiated by the John Hansard Gallery on a wide range of issues relating to the contemporary visual arts and their relationship to broader topics. The idea of exploring issues relating to fine art education, whilst rooted in a specialist, professional field, also grows out of a broader interest in the foundations of fine art production. An examination of the structures by which a formal education system attempts to underpin the activity of professional artists can be seen as fundamental to our understanding of the forces that shape contemporary art. Therefore whilst the papers in this volume will be of interest to those professionally involved in the teaching of fine art in higher education institutions, they will also be of interest to those working in other areas of fine art: artists, critics, curators and arts administrators. We also hope that the arguments presented will have relevance to those involved in higher education in other disciplines.

In fact, the idea of describing someone working in an art school as a professional teacher is somewhat unusual - at least in Britain and until very recently. Traditionally the artist as itinerant teacher was the bedrock of British art education. However, the challenges facing workers in all areas of higher education at present are greater than ever before, and in the areas of fine art senior staff are now required to see themselves as professional academics delivering a service that can be quantified in terms of value delivered to students. At the same time they are required to be research-active practitioners producing measurable output in terms of exhibitions and publications. On the plus side, artists who teach in art schools now have their personal work as artists recognised as valid research. The other side of the coin is that the teaching must meet with measurable standards. Artists who teach in art schools are required to keep abreast of professional developments in the academic world and are subject to any number of appraisal procedures.

This book is based on a conference, held at the University of Southampton on 9th and 10th December 1993 and entitled **The Artist and The Academy: European Perspectives on Today's Fine Art Education**. Our original research in preparing the agenda for the conference and drawing up a list of speakers to invite confirmed what we had feared: that the existing literature on the subject was very scarce and fragmented. It was important, therefore, to focus on a range of topics that presented a broad and coherent landscape, and yet addressed a specific number of points of reference from which particular debates could grow. It was important to create an academic model, so that the debate could focus on matters of substance, rather than on matters of style. It was bound to be affected by any one of a number of contemporary cultural issues that impinge directly on the visual arts (for example, arguments related to the politics of gender or race, cultural hierarchies or the political map) but we felt it timely to try and give emphasis to the rather less considered subject of the politics of place. Such a perspective seemed to us to be a useful addition to those texts that are already available as an introduction to what is an extremely broad subject area. We hope that out of this publication will grow further debates on increasingly specialised areas of the subject, and would not be entirely unhappy if this was generated by a reaction against the terrain that we have mapped here.

Our preliminary discussions centred on the unproblematic way in which many E.U. cultural initiatives, and the rhetoric that supported and surrounded them, presented the concept of European-ness. We saw contributions from other countries in Europe as offering a broadening of the terms for the discussion of fine art education, which in Britain in the recent past has tended to be dominated by purely national considerations because of the dominating influence of government policies in higher education. It is in this context that we invited Kasper König and Thierry de Duve to make contributions, and their different approaches offer quite different perspectives. However, as Iain Biggs points out later on, the concept of European-ness is problematic if we are simply discussing the European Community as a monoculture, and ignore the complex issues of difference that arise as a result of such discussion. Within this discussion we feel that a consideration of the peripheries, both in a literal sense - hence the politics of place - and in terms of difference and dissent, to be of primary importance. Here we recognised that it was not only the issues of Eurocentrism and multi-culturalism and the so-called New Internationalism that were important. There are also issues closer at hand concerning dissenting institutions and their significance for a range of opportunities for the study of fine art. It is in this context that we have included the paper by Alexander Tzonis and Liane Lefaivre **Why Critical Regionalism Today?** Written in 1990 in relation to contemporary architecture, it has a relevance to the concept of critical regionalism and fine art, and including it in this collection of papers seems extremely helpful, although it was not part of the conference.

A second paper that was not part of the original conference is by Susan Hiller and was originally presented at a Tate Gallery conference, **The Curriculum for Fine Art in Higher Education**, also held in 1993. Her plea is for fine art education as the last surviving programme of education for the right side of the brain. Such a plea is set against what appears to be a slow but relentless move in the other direction, and the inclusion of this paper is complemented by Kasper König's description of the programme at the Frankfurt Städelschule. There the call for the bureaucratic structures that attempt to make every aspect of British art education externally and objectively measurable seems to have been avoided.

It is the relationship between art and other things, and thus the relationship between art education and our knowledge of other things, which this book explores. It is the competence of art education to reflect on other realms of knowledge, and of art to define its critical relationship with other subjects, which is the central theme of this book.

The comment in our opening paragraph that formal art education *attempts to underpin* the structure of the professional art world was chosen carefully, and we should remember that Kasper König's paper proposes that "art would go on even if there were no art schools". None of the papers in this collection assumes that the character of the art world of the future can, or should, be the sole responsibility of formal art education. However, this book does make significant claims for art education that cannot be easily reconciled with standard models of vocational training, whatever the level. These claims give fine art education a special importance in wider cultural terms and we hope that this collection of papers will be successful in giving its readers access to some of those wider perspectives.

Two Models of the Fine Art Academy

In 1981 the ICA staged an exhibition entitled **A Continuing Process: The New Creativity in British Art Education 1955-65** (ICA and various venues), which was organised by David Thistlewood and Sandy Nairne. The exhibition celebrated the "revolutionary" changes that had taken place in art education in the period between the end of the Second World War and the beginning of the Seventies. Thistlewood's intention was to give particular emphasis to the new teaching ideas put into practice by three important art educators - Victor Pasmore, Tom Hudson and Richard Hamilton - in the period 1955-65. This celebration in 1981 was a reflection of the fact that their ideas had had a significant influence on the development of art education in the intervening period, and many of the ideas that they brought to art education continue to be of great importance.

Although we can no longer visit the exhibition, the catalogue, written by Thistlewood, remains a vivid commentary on the art-teaching theories associated with these three artists[1]. Their methods owed much to the influence of the Bauhaus experiment, both directly and as celebrated by Herbert Read, notably in **Art and Industry** (1934)[2] and **Education Through Art** (1943)[3]. Pasmore, Hamilton and Hudson, each in his own way, found the institutional power to put into practice new ideas about education that Thistlewood was moved to describe as "liberal, humanist and self-evidently right".

In **Art and Industry** Read quotes from a paper given to a meeting of the Design & Industry Association in 1933 by Walter Gropius, who was director of the Bauhaus from 1919 to 1928. In his paper Gropius described the relationship between the Bauhaus and the larger world thus:

> "Our object was to permeate both types of mind; to liberate the creative artist from his other-worldliness and reintegrate him into the workaday world of realities; and at the same time to broaden and humanise the rigid, almost exclusively material mind of the business man. Our governing conception of the basic unity of all design in its relation to life, which informed all our work, was therefore in diametrical opposition to that of 'art for art's sake', and the even more dangerous philosophy it sprang from: business as an end in itself."[5]

In these sentiments we can detect the modernist utopian drive that enshrines creativity as a key humaniser of social conditions. The focus on creativity as one of the key human attributes that art schools should promote is analysed by Thierry de Duve in his essay **When Form Has Become Attitude - And Beyond**.

The principle that there is a universal human creativity that needs only the right conditions to blossom was a significant presumption in the teaching methods of the three pioneers celebrated in Thistlewood's text in **A Continuing Process**. He writes: "What now exists is a general devotion to the principle of individual creative development - accepting, as a premise, that the multiform results of such an attitude may not be hedged about or limited by preconceptions."

In the next paragraph Thistlewood elaborates: "research into the properties of traditional and modern materials, and into craft practices and modern industrial techniques alike, with the intentions of exploiting any or all of them towards creative ends; analysis of environment according to personal vision; curiosity about 'internal' or 'psychological' determinants of created form: such matters now do not seem misplaced in art education."[6]

Which, then, are the pedagogic principles of the post-Bauhaus approach to art education that are still important to contemporary fine art teaching? This question can be answered by considering the assumptions that lie behind the Pasmore/Hamilton/Hudson approach. In order to particularise the character of their techniques, Thistlewood describes how, on moving to Leicester College of Art, "he [Tom Hudson] proceeded to decategorise the curriculum he found there. While work obviously had to be categorised afterwards for the purpose of criticism, he was careful always during creative exploration to emphasise the individual's ideas, and to encourage the expansion of these across dimensional, material and technical boundaries."[7]

He continues, describing Hudson's pedagogic technique as follows:

> "He now began to argue [that] there could be no anticipation of the student's future creative forms because of differing perceptions and preferences and the resulting, infinite range of formal languages. Because individuals could invent their own languages, it was not the teacher's responsibility to determine whether the work should be abstract or realistic or related to a given project."[8]

In Thistlewood's description of Hudson's methods we can discern the tension between an open, interdisciplinary approach to art education (de-categorised, to use Thistlewood's terminology) and the necessity for the teaching staff to return student work to the categories in order for it to be criticised. In returning the students' work "to the categories" we can see the clear implication that the work is subjected to the authority of the disciplines from which, however exotic the form, it can be seen, finally, to have sprung. The extending of student work in dimensional, material or technical terms clearly follows one of Herbert Read's key definitions of form, "which might be called Platonic, in which form is regarded as a representation of the idea".[9] Indeed, it has been an underlying assumption of art in the modern period that form, to a significant extent, has consequences for content.

Thistlewood is at pains to emphasise that the pedagogic intention is to keep the issue of the means (material, form etc) an open question for the students - and to allow meaning to flow from their materials and making process. This making process, he suggests, results not in an entry by the students into language (in the singular) - some sense of meaning-making that is communal - but the simultaneous creation of languages in the plural. When artefacts are produced by the students as a consequence of these investigations the expectation is ("obviously" according to Thistlewood) that the work will be returned "to the categories". What follows the making process is that the art teacher places the students' work in its categories, and in so doing, mediates between the competing languages that the students invent. In other words, the teacher is the one person who is in a position to judge between the competing visual languages, and who can determine which communicate and are thus valid, important, meaningful.

In the return of the student's work to its category one can see that what is guaranteed is the subjection of the student's work to a critical framework that is determined by the teacher (and which might well be informed by the pre-existing tenets of the academic). Whatever the cast of the teacher's mind - and one cannot but doubt that Hudson had an extremely sharp and open intelligence when it came to offering criticism - we can see that the organisation of the class results in very particular terms for the interpretation, and judgement, of the student's work (an outcome that could be seen as the opposite of the intention of modernist theorising about new art production where the flirtation with the void of non-language is constantly evoked). This is not only to reinforce the hold that the knowledgeable critic has on the attribution of meaning, but it also recoups the master/disciple relationship. The teaching regime places the teacher in the key position of being able to exercise the power of interpretation over the student's work. Thus the teacher is in the ambivalent position of enabling the students and, at the same time, guaranteeing the retention of authority for him or herself. First there is a push towards personal autonomy by the students - encouraged by the teacher's rhetoric of freedom - then there is a pulling back as the teacher retrieves authority for the critical process. There is, as a consequence, a constant tension in the teaching between personal liberation and the constraints of categories and the implications of discipline.

In this short description by Thistlewood we see perfectly exemplified the double bind that is so characteristic of the modern fine art academy: the tensions between discipline/liberation and authority/autonomy. First the art academy must teach, yet it expects its students to resist slavish adherence to academic tenets: this is the transgressive principle of modernism. Then there is an attempt to retrieve authority. Transgression, modernism's tactical assumption of constant radicality, is reluctantly institutionalised. From this tradition springs the Transgressive model of the art academy.

However, the fine art academy is also the site of redemptive play and the drive to encourage universal human creativity. Art school teaching that proposes art-making as a subversion of capitalist production also proposes "a redefinition of the avant-garde in terms of resistance rather than transgression"[10]. Ideas of this kind have also had an effect on the pedagogic environment. The recuperation of human sociability through the enhancement of creativity and the application of creativity to all aspects of human existence (these can readily be seen as forms of resistance) we might see as the project of the Theraputic model of the art academy.

(In these observations of the existence of two models of the academy, a debt must be acknowledged to the observations that Iain Biggs offers in his essay **Peripheral Vision**).

It seems clear that the relationship between the artist and the academy is determined by the way these two models are utilised in the practical business of running a school. These two models lie, as fundamental assumptions, behind the changes that have swept through British art schools in the twenty years since the second (1970)

Coldstream Report. The diagrams accompanying the text are attempts to summarise the characteristics of both models, and of their operation. It can be seen that the consequences of each model are quite different.

First, the Transgressive model. When we see elements of this model being enacted, we will find that the education is organised around an expectation that the students' work will express radical individuation. Their work will be valued because it breaks accepted conventions: it must not conform to existing prescriptions for the appearance of the art object. The Transgressive Academy is pragmatic in many of its operations, encouraging all aspects of professionalism: commitment, professional knowledge, appropriate attention to the technical requirements of making. The student experiences the process of individuation through the rejection of specific elements of the received professional wisdom, as enshrined (however imperfectly) in the institution. Even though transgression is the founding principle of the Transgressive Academy, it is feared by the institution, not only as a declaration of differentiation, but also as a threat to the generalised sense of the status quo that the institution represents. There is often a fearful expectation of this repudiation amongst the teachers - an expectation that can drive them to authoritarian extremes (largely ineffectual) in their teaching. Younger members of the teaching staff will often go to great lengths to avoid being the personal focus of this repudiation. To do this they will repudiate their own institutional role by finding some sense of solidarity with the students.

In the Transgressive Academy what is exposed is the expectation that everything one can say about work has already started down the road to being a convention. We will observe also that in the Transgressive Academy the progress of the programme is similar to induction into a guild. The expectation is that the students must, in some way, offer radical difference, not only from earlier generations of artists but also from their peers; achieving this is, ultimately, the sign of their guild membership.

On the other hand, were we to find the pure Therapeutic model in operation we would discover a curious psychoanalytic institution. Here

A MODEL OF THE FINE ART ACADEMY No 1 –
THE CHARACTERISTICS OF THE PURE TRANSGRESSIVE MODEL

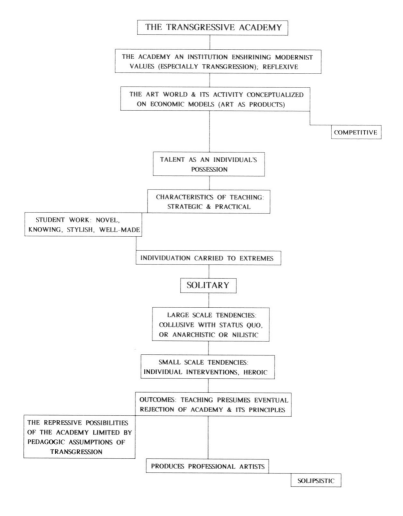

THE TRANSGRESSIVE ACADEMY

THE ACADEMY AN INSTITUTION ENSHRINING MODERNIST
VALUES (ESPECIALLY TRANSGRESSION); REFLEXIVE

THE ART WORLD & ITS ACTIVITY CONCEPTUALIZED
ON ECONOMIC MODELS (ART AS PRODUCTS)

COMPETITIVE

TALENT AS AN INDIVIDUAL'S
POSSESSION

CHARACTERISTICS OF TEACHING:
STRATEGIC & PRACTICAL

STUDENT WORK: NOVEL,
KNOWING, STYLISH, WELL-MADE

INDIVIDUATION CARRIED TO EXTREMES

SOLITARY

LARGE SCALE TENDENCIES:
COLLUSIVE WITH STATUS QUO,
OR ANARCHISTIC OR NILISTIC

SMALL SCALE TENDENCIES:
INDIVIDUAL INTERVENTIONS, HEROIC

OUTCOMES: TEACHING PRESUMES EVENTUAL
REJECTION OF ACADEMY & ITS PRINCIPLES

THE REPRESSIVE POSSIBILITIES
OF THE ACADEMY LIMITED BY
PEDAGOGIC ASSUMPTIONS OF
TRANSGRESSION

PRODUCES PROFESSIONAL ARTISTS

SOLIPSISTIC

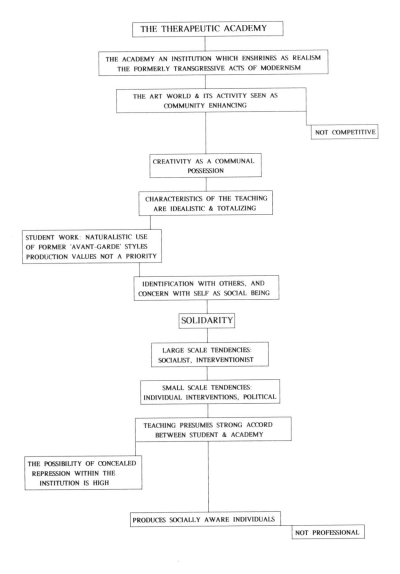

A MODEL OF THE FINE ART ACADEMY No 2 –
THE CHARACTERISTICS OF THE PURE THERAPEUTIC MODEL

THE THERAPEUTIC ACADEMY

THE ACADEMY AN INSTITUTION WHICH ENSHRINES AS REALISM
THE FORMERLY TRANSGRESSIVE ACTS OF MODERNISM

THE ART WORLD & ITS ACTIVITY SEEN AS
COMMUNITY ENHANCING

NOT COMPETITIVE

CREATIVITY AS A COMMUNAL
POSSESSION

CHARACTERISTICS OF THE TEACHING
ARE IDEALISTIC & TOTALIZING

STUDENT WORK: NATURALISTIC USE
OF FORMER 'AVANT-GARDE' STYLES
PRODUCTION VALUES NOT A PRIORITY

IDENTIFICATION WITH OTHERS, AND
CONCERN WITH SELF AS SOCIAL BEING

SOLIDARITY

LARGE SCALE TENDENCIES:
SOCIALIST, INTERVENTIONIST

SMALL SCALE TENDENCIES:
INDIVIDUAL INTERVENTIONS, POLITICAL

TEACHING PRESUMES STRONG ACCORD
BETWEEN STUDENT & ACADEMY

THE POSSIBILITY OF CONCEALED
REPRESSION WITHIN THE
INSTITUTION IS HIGH

PRODUCES SOCIALLY AWARE INDIVIDUALS

NOT PROFESSIONAL

there are no conflicts between teachers and students: disruptions would be psychological "problems", if there were any. There is, to be sure, transgression within the Therapeutic Academy, but it is domesticated as just one more clinical (and, thus, pedagogic) tool. It has a tendency to regard transgressive behaviour as regressive. This is the concerned, responsible institution enabling better people, better communities, through the power of enhanced creativity, expressed as art. It is overtly political and necessarily socialist.

In this model of the academy some of the things that are given high value in the Transgressive Academy are little valued. Originality is less valued than appropriateness, where appropriateness is measured by social consensus. Skill and finish are likewise given low priority where their presence might be used to discriminate between practitioners.

Of course, although their hidden Platonic presences underlie the rhetoric of contemporary fine art teaching, no fine art academy employs either of these models unalloyed by the other. Experience suggests that it is usual for teaching teams to utilise aspects of both models in a sort of ad hoc mixed economy. However, it is not unusual to discover that there is no member of the academic staff with a clear picture of the overall implications of their particular hybrid. This means that the staff have little grasp of the potential they have for subjecting their students to a contradictory value system that is created by the conflation of educational strategies drawing on both models. Here we find the most malignant occurrence of the art teacher as the creator of categories and the referee of languages.

Perhaps the time has come for today's fine art education to recognise these two models as its heritage. They are the source of its continuing inconsistencies and, where used positively (to allow for the creation of alternative spaces), its richness.

Finally, it seems inevitable that the tensions between the Transgressive and the Therapeutic models can be discerned, implicitly or explicitly, in much that is discussed in the papers in this book.

NOTES

1   David Thistlewood, **A Continuing Process** (Institute of Contemporary Arts, London, 1981).

2   Herbert Read, **Art And Industry** (Faber and Faber, London, 1934).

3   Herbert Read, **Education Through Art** (Faber and Faber, London, 1943).

4   David Thistlewood, op. cit., p. 6.

5   Walter Gropius. The paper was reprinted in the **Journal of the Royal Institute of British Architects** (May 1934).

6   David Thistlewood, op. cit., p. 6

7   Thistlewood David, Op cit p. 40.

8   The same insight that crossing/breaking the categories/ disciplines of fine art can liberate creativity is one that is explored in **The Interdisciplinary Field of Fine Art** later in this book. It is noted there that the concept is promoted as the more radical strand of the 1970 Coldstream Report and, indeed, Thistlewood reports that Hudson, Hamilton, Pasmore and "their ideas had direct and indirect representation to the Coldstream Commission" (p. 10).

9   Herbert Read, **Art Now** (Faber and Faber, London, 1933) p. 90.

10 Hal Foster, **Recodings: Art, Spectacle, Cultural Politics** (Bay Press, Seattle, USA, 1987, p. 7).

II

WHEN FORM HAS BECOME ATTITUDE - AND BEYOND

Thierry de Duve

It used to be that the teaching of art was academic and proud of it. Rooted in the observation of nature and the imitation of previous art, the long apprenticeship of a would-be painter or sculptor was primarily an acquisition of skills put under specific cultural constraints. Life-drawing and its underlying discourse, anatomy, provided the basic skill ennobled with humanistic knowledge. Never, though, was art equated with skill. What deserved admiration in the accomplished artist was talent, not craftsmanship. Skill could be acquired, talent could not, since talent was thought of as a gift of nature - a gift, however, which could neither develop nor express itself outside the rules, conventions, and codes provided by the tradition. Tradition set the standards against which the production of art students was measured. Academic teaching had great ambitions as regards the maintenance of tradition and the passing on of quality standards; it had little vanity as regards its ability to "turn out" individual artists. All it could hope to do was nurture and discipline its students' gifts within the limits of nature's generosity, and to grant even the most ungifted students a technical know-how capable of securing them a recognised, if humble, place in society and a plausible, if modest, source of income. Between the work of the artisan and that of the genius the Academy recognized a leap in quality, but also the cultural continuity of one and the same trade in which everybody held his (or her) rank.

All this was destroyed in less than a century. Reynolds was probably the last great academic pedagogue; a century after him, the Academy had withered into academicism. As industrialisation and the social upheaval, scientific progress and ideological transformations that went with it decomposed the hitherto stable social fabric and, on the whole, more or less destroyed all craftsmanship, the examples of the past lost their credibility, in art and elsewhere, and the chain of tradition was eventually broken. To the sensitive artist, academic art and training became just that, academic, and the new art began to look toward the future for its legitimation, with fear and hope alike. The avant-garde was launched. Painting and sculpture, progressively turning away from observation and imitation of outside models, turned inwards and started to observe and imitate their very means of expression. Instead of exerting their talent within relatively fixed conventions, the modernist artists put those conventions themselves to an aesthetic test and, one by one, discarded those by which they no longer felt constrained. Excellence in art came to be measured against the resistance of the medium, with, as yardstick, the honesty with which the artist yields to it. All tradition rejected, painting came to be seen as a sort of essence, present in all painting, past, present or future, as if the medium in its purity could set the rules by itself, command over skill, and provide a vessel for talent. Sculpture, architecture, photography, even cinema became similar essences.

Soon, art schooling was affected by the avant-garde. As the examples and standards of the past could no longer be trusted, as imitation and observation could no longer provide the basics for the apprenticeship of art, the teaching of art had to look elsewhere for roots in both nature and culture. This it achieved in two ways. The figure of Man - the universal measure of all things in nature - was relinquished as outer model for observation, but was recouped as inner subjective principle. Psychology replaced anatomy in its function as foundational discourse for a new artistic humanism. The new doctrine stated that all men are endowed with innate faculties which it is the function of education to allow to grow. Thus, specialisation in the visual arts meant the specific training and growth of the faculties of visual perception and imagination. How to train them became the pedagogical issue. Again, psychology, - not the introspective kind but perception psychology, *Gestalt* theory, and so on - provided the idea that the ability to perceive is, by nature, already cultural, that perception is, so to speak, a basic reading skill. It followed from there that imagination was a basic writing skill of sorts. "Creativity" is the name, the modern name, given to the combined innate faculties of perception and imagination. Everybody is endowed with it, and the closer it remains to sheer, blank endowment, the greater is its potential. A child, a primitive, has more creativity than a cultivated adult. The ideal art student, the artist of the future, came to be dreamt of as an infant whose natural ability to read and write the visual world needs only to be properly tutored. The problem became to find the appropriate means. If only the practice of painting and sculpture could be broken into semantic "atoms", if only some elementary visual alphabet and syntax could be set up, then art - art itself, not merely skill - could be taught and taught without resorting to a now obsolete tradition. Talent, as such, no longer exists. It lies in a raw state in everyone's creativity, and skill lies, so to speak, ready-made in the properties of the medium: in the linearity of drawing, in the two-dimensionality of the picture plane, in the volumetric properties of sculpture. In principle, if not in fact, the learning of art became simple: students should learn how to tap their unspoilt creativity, guided by immediate feeling and emotion, and to read their medium, obeying its immanent syntax. As their aesthetic sensibility and artistic literacy progressed, their ability to feel and to read would translate into the ability to express and to articulate. Nurtured perception and imagination would produce artworks of a new kind.

This pedagogical programme proved to be a self-fulfilling prophecy. All progressive pedagogues of this century, from Froebel to Montessori to Decroly; all school reformers and philosophers of education, from Rudolf Steiner to John Dewey, have based their projects and programmes on creativity, or rather, on the belief in creativity, on the conviction that creativity - not tradition, not rules and conventions - is the best starting point for education. Moreover, all great modern theorists of art, from Herbert Read to E. H. Gombrich to Rudolph Arnheim, have entertained similar convictions and devoted considerable energy to breaking up the "visual language" into its basic components and demonstrating the universality of its perceptive and psychological "laws". And finally, needless to say, there is not one pioneer of Modernist art, from Malevich to Kandinsky and Klee, or from Itten and Moholy-Nagy to Albers and Hofmann, who has not been actively involved in the creation of art schools and teaching programmes based on the reduction of practice to the fundamental elements of a syntax immanent to the medium. Kandinsky wrote **Von Punkt zur Linie zur Fläche** in 1924, and since then every art school in the world has a 2-D and a 3-D studio to prepare its students for painting and sculpture. If they had been strictly faithful to Kandinsky, if they had also taken their cue from Cubism, they would have a 1-D and a 4-D studio as well.

My point is not just to be ironic, and certainly not to dismiss this philosophy without further trial, but merely to stress that a philosophy it is, a biased one and a dated one. Let's call it the Bauhaus model. It was never carried out with the radical purity of my description, not even at the Bauhaus itself, which died under the pressure of its own contradictions as much as it did under the hand of the Nazis. But the Bauhaus model, more or less amended, more or less debased, has set a series of assumptions about art teaching upon which dozens of art and architecture schools around the world have been built, and which are, as of today, still underlying, often subliminally, almost unconsciously, most art curriculums, including (if I'm well informed), a great number of foundation courses across the U.K. Moreover, it is seemingly the only model that pits itself coherently against the old academic model, such as it also survives, equally amended and often degenerated beyond recognition, not just in the very few Ecoles de Beaux-Arts that still defend it (actually, I don't know of any that still do), but also in the immense majority of art schools and academies around the world that seek to find a compromise between traditionalism and modernism.

I have sketched out an oversimplified picture, a caricature, even, of the postulates underlying the teaching of art up to recent years. But a caricature is all the more truthful in that it is exaggerated, and I will not hesitate in exaggerating it even more forcibly, in order to make those postulates appear as postulates - that is, as mere postulates. Two models, even though in reality they contaminate each other, divide up the teaching of art conceptually. On the one hand, there is the academic model; on the other, there is the Bauhaus model. The former believes in talent, the latter in creativity. The former classifies the arts according to techniques, what I would call the *métier*; the latter according to the medium. The former fosters imitation; the latter invention. Both models are obsolete. The academic model entered a deep crisis as soon as it began to deserve the derogative label of academicism. Its decadence was accomplished under the pressure of modern art, which is why no return to the past is thinkable lest the blackout is pronounced on all the art and all the artists of modernity. The Bauhaus model also entered an open crisis. That phenomenon is more recent but it isn't new, dating from the Sixties, I would say. It, too, goes hand in hand with the art of its time, and it is contemporaneous with the deep loss of confidence that modernism has undergone since those years. Now, it is dramatic to have to teach according to postulates one doesn't believe in anymore. But in order to change them, one has to see them clearly. Let's review the evidence: do we have to choose between talent and creativity, between *métier* and medium?

Talent vs Creativity

The difference between talent and creativity is that the former is unequally distributed and the latter universally. In the passage from one word to the other, there is of course a complete reversal of ideologies, and it is not difficult to see that, historically, the progress of the ideology of creativity went hand in hand with that of the idea of democracy and of egalitarianism. The use of the word creativity in this elevated sense itself is relatively recent, but its germs were already present in the Romantic notion of the genius. Creativity is grounded in a utopian belief summarised by a slogan that repeats itself with clockwork regularity throughout the history of modernity, from Rimbaud to Beuys: everyone an artist. Of course, it always meant : everyone is potentially an artist. Talent is also a potential but, on the one hand, it does not depend on some psychology of the faculties, and on the other, it is inseparable from the specific terrain where it is exerted, which in the last resort is always technical. One has talent for music, for carpentry or for cookery, but not talent in general. Creativity, by contrast, is conceived as an absolute and unformalised potential, a supply of energy prior to any division of labour. One has creativity, without qualification; one is creative, period.

Three major consequences derive from this for any art-educational project based on creativity. The first is that nothing should, in principle, restrict access to the study of art. The second is that art itself, and not just the technical means of art, can be taught. And the third is that initiation to art in general should precede every specialisation (that was the role of the *Grundkurs*, or foundation course, at the Bauhaus). The contradiction between these principles is blatant: many art schools yield to the particularly perverse illusion (which, moreover, frequently backfires) that they produce or fabricate artists, while at the same time considering that their incoming students are artists already, even though only potentially. In fact, all teachers know by experience that talent exists and that creativity is a myth. On this point, the Academy saw things a lot more clearly than modernity. The myth is generous, and this is not a negligible quality when it comes to teaching. And as long as the myth functions, why denounce it? The problem is that it doesn't function anymore.

Métier vs Medium

The difference between *métier* and medium is that the former has a historical existence and the latter a transhistorical existence. The Academy classified the fine arts according to the *métier* and everything the notion entails: specialised skills, artisan habits, sleights of hand, rules of composition, canons of beauty, in short, a specific tradition. Modernism classifies the arts according to the medium and everything this notion entails: particular materials, supports, tools, gestures, technical procedures, and conventions of specificity. That an artist practised the *métier* of painter meant that he belonged to the guild of painters and had a place in a given affiliation. His definition of painting would have been, simply: what painters do. That an artist works in the medium of painting means that he questions painting for what it has to say about itself and hasn't said yet. His definition of painting might be: what no painter has done yet. The *métier* gets practised, the medium gets questioned; the *métier* gets transmitted, the medium communicates or gets communicated, the *métier* gets learnt, the medium gets discovered; the *métier* is a tradition, the medium is a language; the *métier* rests on experience, the medium relies on experimentation. From the former to the latter, a reversal occurred in the conception of history. The *métier* is always received from the past; even when regulated by ideals that are supposedly eternal, those ideals are situated upstream in history (like the antique). The medium is received from nowhere; it purports to actualise transcendentals, that is, *a priori* conditions of possibility, which, regulating the work, should lead to the revelation of the medium's essence, paradoxically situated downstream in history. Thus, for the academic model, to teach painting means to transmit its legacy and to allow the apprentice to find a place in a chain of affiliation of which he has a strong awareness and which he will have to pursue. For the Bauhaus model, to teach painting is to open access to a being called painting, supposedly immanent to all paintings from all times, but whose ultimate revelation is yet to come; it is to invite the student to subtract from the medium and thereby to subtract himself from the chain of affiliation.

Three major consequences derive from this. First, teaching the arts according to the medium cultivates distrust of technical skill because mastering the medium gets in the way of questioning the medium; what matters is not technical apprenticeship but the discovery of those qualities that can be deduced from the medium itself. Second, in cutting off the arts from their specific affiliations and reorganising them according to the specificity of their perceptive properties, this teaching denies itself the possibility of conceiving that there is art in between the mediums. And third, it seeks to teach the future, which is of course impossible. The verdict should be more severe, even, for the myth of the medium than it was for the myth of creativity, with which, moreover, it is contradictory under certain aspects. It has had considerable pedagogical efficiency, but its perverse effects now outrun its benefits.

Imitation vs Invention

The difference between imitation and invention goes without saying. Whereas imitation reproduces, invention produces; whereas imitation generates sameness, invention generates otherness; whereas imitation seeks continuity, invention seeks novelty. The Academy was aware that artists worthy of the name invent. However, even though academic teaching spotted a sign of a student's talent in his capacity to invent, it was not on his capacity to invent that it judged him, nor was it through stimulating invention that it claimed to educate him. Quite the contrary. It was through imposing on him imitation, invention's antithesis : the imitation of nature, of the Ancients, of the master. The Bauhaus model, by contrast, fosters invention, because every progress in its expression indicates a liberation of the student's creativity, an actualisation of his artistic potential. The abandonment of naturalism, the break with the Ancients, the rejection of the master are the predictable results. Now, that a teaching system should systematically encourage the rejection of the master isn't without contradiction. Creativity being the source of invention, the medium its target, the teacher - who is no longer a master - owes his authority to the very constraints of the medium while he invites the student to transgress the medium's limits in order to prove his creativity. He sees it as his task to detect the student's invention and to value it for its own sake, while referring it to the medium and interpreting it within the limits of the medium's specificity.

Again, three major consequences derive from this. First, the kind of teaching that seeks to provoke invention tends to judge its students on a quasi-quantitative basis, on the basis of the frequency of invention as such, of its novelty, of its discontinuous and randomlike character, of its unforeseen freshness: all qualities that are real in an accomplished work of art but quite unsuitable when it comes to recording the students' progress. Second, such teaching systematically encourages the students to experiment with the medium, while containing their experimentation within boundaries that are seen not just as a terrain for apprenticeship, but as the limits of the field of practice itself. Finally, such teaching is loath to discuss the content of the students' work and cultivates formalism. These are the cumulative effects of the generosity of the ideology of creativity, and of a conception of the history of art that banks on the future for its legitimation. The trouble is that the myth of creativity is suspicious, and that the future, from which the Bauhaus model expected its legitimation, belongs to our past.

In view of this cursory analysis, it may seem that I promote some return to the academic model of teaching. Not so, of course. In fact, I don't promote anything, not in this paper, anyway. My only intention is to gain a clearer view of the decline of the Bauhaus model, which is far more important for the proper understanding of the present crisis than the long-accomplished demise of the Academy. It is because the paradigm underlying the Bauhaus model, the creativity-medium-invention paradigm, still operates in most art schools, even in those - especially in those, I should say - that consciously bathe in its critique; it is because its three postulates are either inscribed in the structure of the institution, or linger more or less consciously in the heads of the teachers and of the students, that its perverse effects are so pervasive. Whether creativity exists or whether it is merely a useful illusion is for all practical purposes irrelevant as long as it works. Whether there is such a thing as a "visual language" specific to the medium or whether it is merely a pedagogical strategy is equally irrelevant as long as it works. The question is: does the Bauhaus model still work? Is it still useful?

We, who teach in art schools, all have mitigated answers to this, I'm sure. Who among us hears the word creativity without wearing an ironic smile? Who among us still dreams of a utopian visual language à la Kandinsky, some Esperanto composed of red squares, yellow triangles and blue circles? Who still believes in the purity or the specificity of the medium, in the manner of Greenberg? Who, perhaps with Warhol in mind, or Toroni, or Richter, or Steve Reich, will deny that as much contemporary art of quality has been produced through repetition as through invention? If the Bauhaus model still works, perhaps it is in spite of itself. Many of us have grown to value the perverse effects of a teaching method organised, if only nominally, in terms of the purity of the media and the separateness of the disciplines. Many of us have grown to praise the subversive students who do not behave as if they tapped the unspoilt creativity with which they are supposedly endowed, but who, instead, tap the pop culture with which they come equipped. Those of us who teach the "basic" courses know all too well that they can communicate only rules and conventions, and that significant art is art that overthrows, displaces, abandons or subverts rules and conventions. Who has not dreamt, if only secretly, of having students - the best students - forcing the teacher to give them an A+ because they transgressed the rules of the assignment so intelligently that they displayed a perfect awareness of what art-making is about? Those of us who teach "mixed media", "intermedia", "multi-media", or "experimental media" - whatever the name is of the no man's land that most art schools have ended up institutionalising as if it were a medium of its own - know all too well that if they did not assign subject matter or set technical constraints, formal limits, severe deadlines or whatever rules or conventions, they would not achieve much more than organised escapism. The fruits that the Bauhaus tree yielded and still yields are strange hybrids. We all know that. We have come to expect it, even foster it. The last art school with a strict Bauhaus ideology (though already considerably amended) was the Black Mountain College, and its best "fruit" was Rauschenberg. Meanwhile, the Bauhaus itself, with all those great artists teaching there, did not produce a single student of a stature equal to that of the masters. Meanwhile, the most "advanced" art schools are those that, consciously entertaining this grim and disillusioned view of the Bauhaus legacy, openly bank on the perversions - they say the subversion - of this modernist model. The artists they produce - for they produce artists indeed - are people whose criterion is the derision of all the notions derived from that of creativity, such as originality and authenticity, without, for all that, necessarily displaying more talent; people who have pushed the rejection of both the *métier* and the medium to the point where their only technique is the appropriation of ready-mades or people who, through simulation, succeed in denying imitation and invention at the same time.

Such is the present situation. A paradigm has imploded, and though it might be that we are in the midst of a "paradigm shift" (if so, it will be for our successors to see it), what I believe is apparently organising the most advanced art schools is in fact the disenchanted, perhaps nihilistic, after-image of the old Bauhaus paradigm. Let me quickly review the evidence in relation to both the postulates of the academic model, talent-*métier*-imitation, and those of the Bauhaus model, creativity-medium-invention. What seems to have taken their place is a new triad of notions: attitude-practice-deconstruction.

Talent and Creativity vs Attitude

In the wake of the student upheaval of the late Sixties no one was ready to admit the inequality of talent, out of fear of seeming irredeemably reactionary. But the May '68 slogan, "all power to the imagination", didn't last very long, and soon creativity lost its aura, too. Philosophically speaking, the times were very suspicious of anything more or less resembling the old psychology of the faculties, and creativity, which is a neo-Romantic amalgam of the Kantian faculties of sensibility and imagination, became old hat. It had everything against itself: being universal, it could only be "bourgeois"; being transcendental, it could only be "metaphysical"; being natural, it could only be "ideological". But its greatest sin was that it could not be willed, and the most progressive art and art teaching of the Seventies thought that art had to be willed, whether it aligned itself with some political programme bathed in revolutionary rhetorics, or whether it saw itself as the relentless critique of the dominant ideology. Anyway, it had become hard to suppose that creativity was the potential of mankind in general, and equally hard to hope that it could be instilled through propaganda or education (think of Joseph Beuys, in this context: he certainly represents the last great and tragic hero of the modern myth of creativity, immolating himself on the altar of both pedagogy and "social sculpture"). Thus another concept took the place of creativity, that of "attitude". A concept that is a blank, actually: a sort of zero degree of psychology, a neutral point amidst ideological choices, a volition without content.

Of course, in order to be progressive - and how could art of any significance not be progressive? - attitude had to be critical. Lukács, Adorno, Althusser and others were called in to tell would-be artists that neither talent nor creativity were needed to make art but, instead, that "critical attitude" was mandatory. And the fact that not just artists but all "cultural workers" were thought to be in need of a critical attitude of course helped to shape a new, strongly politicised discourse about art and its relation to society, a discourse that, throughout the Seventies and part of the Eighties, became the dominant discourse, not in all art schools, admittedly, but certainly in the most progressive, the most avant-gardistic or - why not say it? - the most fashionable ones. Even if you turn to less politicised aspects of the dominant discourse about art in those years you will see the central position of the notion of attitude confirmed. It is towards the end of the Sixties that the concept of "aesthetic attitude" surfaced in art theory, thanks to Jerome Stolnitz in particular, but also, I should say, thanks to Duchamp's growing reputation as the first conceptual artist, a combination of influences that greatly helped in pushing aside aesthetics while retaining the notion of attitude. Finally - and this, I believe, clinches it, if only symbolically - it was in 1969 that Harald Szeemann organised the famous exhibition **When Attitudes Become Form**, at the Kunsthalle in Bern. Both the date and the title coined for this exhibition are symptomatic, for it was then and there that conceptual art was acknowledged for the first time by a major art institution (MoMA was to follow before long with the **Information** show, in 1970), providing a new model for advanced art soon to be emulated and disseminated by most art schools.

Everybody here, I'm sure, is familiar with what happened next. Linguistics, semiotics, anthropology, psychoanalysis, Marxism, feminism, structuralism and post-structuralism, in short, "theory" (or so-called "French theory") entered art schools and succeeded in displacing - sometimes replacing - studio practice while renewing the critical vocabulary and intellectual tools with which to approach the making and the appreciating of art. With considerable differences depending on national and local circumstances (the Anglo-Saxon world having the lead), this shift - whose first aspect is the shift from creativity to attitude - occurred in the mid- to late Seventies and was a *fait accompli* by the mid-Eighties. By then, to take just a few prominent examples, the Nova Scotia College of Art and Design in Halifax had its most prolific period behind itself, Cal Arts was launching a generation of successful alumni, and Goldsmiths' was the place to be. In those days attitude still had to be critical, which basically meant: critical of the social and political status quo. But soon the very success of these art schools began attracting students who went there because of the instant rewards they were seemingly able to promise them. For these students (with or without the conscious or unconscious complicity of their teachers, I can't tell), what had started as an ideological alternative to both talent and creativity, called "critical attitude", became just that, an attitude, a stance, a pose, a contrivance. This phenomenon, of course, widely exceeds the few art schools I just named; it even exceeds art schools in general, for it is rampant throughout the whole academic world, especially in the humanities. It can be summarised by saying that political commitment sank into political correctness. Meanwhile, what remains of the old postulates - the academic postulate called talent and the modernist postulate called creativity - on which to ground a plausible art curriculum is the poorest, the most tautological notion of all: that of an artist's attitude.

Métier and Medium vs Practice

Dividing the arts according to the medium rather than to the *métier*; reading art history in terms of "a progressive surrender to the resistance of its medium" (Clement Greenberg); fostering the purity of the medium as a value in itself are the three strong points of formalist criticism and modernist doctrine in art. As is well known, formalism and modernism have been under heavy fire since the mid-Sixties, first in America, soon after in England, and then in the rest of the Western world. Just as with Harald Szeemann's show, **When Attitudes Become**

Form, let me choose a symbolic event to pinpoint this, an event all the more symbolic in that it happened in 1966 at an art school. John Latham was a part-time instructor at St. Martin's, in London, when he borrowed Clement Greenberg's **Art and Culture** from the school's library and, with the complicity of Barry Flanagan, then a student at St. Martin's, organised an event entitled **Still & Chew**, when a number of pages of the book were chewed by the participants and spat into a jar, then submitted to a complex chemical treatment. You know the aftermath of this performance (or was it a happening?): a year or so later, when asked to return the book to the library, John Latham returned it indeed, but in the shape of a jar containing the unspeakable, let alone unreadable, mixture. He was fired the next day.

Today, needless to say, he could do the same performance with the principal's blessing, and the librarian wouldn't even bother to reorder **Art and Culture**. Events, happenings, and performances have long been absorbed into art schools, and even though most schools keep a painting studio, a sculpture studio, a printmaking studio, and so on, they have added to the list a "mixed media", an "interdisciplinary", or a "free-for-all" studio - whatever the name - which definitely indicates that the teaching of art no longer rests on an aesthetic commitment to the specificity or the purity of the medium. By 1970 Clement Greenberg and Michael Fried were already the last art critics to uphold the idea that no art of significance could be done that sits in between media, and that if something is neither painting nor sculpture, then it is not art. Against them, a whole generation of conceptual artists were relying on Duchamp in order to maintain that the art was in the concept, that it was dematerialised, that it did not cling to any medium, above all not to painting. They fought against the medium but, of course, didn't rehabilitate the *métier* for all that. Just as with the word "attitude", what was soon to replace both the *métier* and the medium was another magical word, "practice".

By 1975, the word "practice" was widely in use among all the people who had been in touch with "French theory", and since "French theory", after all, originated in France, it is there, in the writings of the

Tel Quel people, in particular, that it acquired a cluster of interesting meanings in the context of literature and art. One of its benefits was that it was charged with prestigious political connotations, Marxist, of course, and Althusserian. More important is that it is a general word not a specific one, or, to say this differently, that it puts the emphasis on the social, not on the technical, division of labour. Applied to painting, for example, it allowed us to conceive of painting not in terms of a specific skill (such as entailed by the notion of *métier*, nor in terms of a specific medium (such as the Greenbergian flatness), but in terms of a specific historical institution called "pictorial practice". This is the way both the painters belonging to the Support-Surface group, and their arch-enemy, Daniel Buren, used the word in defence of painting. Other artists, who were defending interdisciplinarity against specificity, began speaking of "artistic practice" or "practices", depending on whether the generic was thought of as being one or plural. But the most interesting - i.e. symptomatic - phenomenon is that the word art itself (simply, art) became taboo. It was guilty of conveying some faith in the "essence" of art, I mean, in the existence of some transhistorical and transcultural common denominator among all artistic practices. Our epoch being radically relativistic, it wouldn't allow such unorthodox belief. The orthodoxy of the times prescribed - and still prescribe - conceiving of art as being just one "signifying practice" (that expression was coined by Julia Kristeva) among others.

I have just said: "prescribed - and still prescribe". In fact, I'm not so sure. One of the things I expect from this conference is that it may help me understand to what extent the orthodoxy of discourse (what I nastily referred to as political correctness) fails to hide the reality of anxieties, disappointments, shattered beliefs, which, I suspect, have a hard time expressing themselves without giving the impression (as I most probably do) of wanting to go backwards and resorting to nostalgia. I hope that the discussion will bring these difficulties into the open, but meanwhile I would like to stress that what was in the Seventies an avant-gardistic discourse has, by now, been largely institutionalised. I know of at least one art school where the students have the choice of enrolling either in "Communication" or in "Artistic

Practice". As always, the magic of changing names is a symptom: the expression "artistic practice" has become a ritual formula, conveying the vague suspicion that has come to surround the word art, while failing to designate referents in the world (that is, actual works) of which one could be sure that the word art has ceased to apply to them significantly.

Imitation and Invention vs Deconstruction

When the culture that fosters invention starts to doubt, it ceases to oppose itself to the culture fostering imitation that it claimed to supplant. Conversely, when the absence of models to be imitated begins to be felt as a loss and no longer as a liberation, this can only mean that this culture's capacity to invent without looking back has dried up. Once this point is reached (and God knows it has been reached: look at all the neo- and all the post-movements; look at the endemic practices of quotation, second-or third-degree self-referentiality, replicas, and the like), then it is no longer enough to say that imitation repeats and that invention makes the difference. The very concepts of repetition and difference ought to be thought anew, transversally, so to speak. Towards the end of the Sixties, again, and sitting on the uneasy boundary between literature and philosophy, Jacques Derrida, but also Gilles Deleuze and others, began thinking about difference and repetition together. Between the live voice creating newness and the trace that supplants and supplements the missing origin, they showed the link dismantling their expected opposition. Derrida sought *écriture* in creation and *différance* in reproduction, while Deleuze showed that the eternal return of sameness inhabited the production of difference. Traditional concepts such as presence versus absence, immediacy versus mediation, originality versus secondarity, were no longer secure oppositions, and had to be deconstructed.

The success of deconstruction is not simply explained - let alone explained away - by the quality of the philosophical work done under its name, and even less so by the mere influence of Derrida - and of Paul de Man on the other side of the Atlantic - on literary criticism. If it had not resonated at a very precise stage in the crisis of modernity, it would not have achieved success at all. But, as we all know, it has, to the point where deconstructionism - and that's the last straw, really - became the banner under which an architecture movement developed, after having invaded art criticism and, more recently, the teaching of art itself. Rather misunderstood and badly assimilated, deconstruction has apparently become, in the eighties, a method by which to produce art and to teach it. As such, however, rather misunderstood and badly assimilated, deconstruction is merely the symptom of the disarray of a generation of art teachers who have lived through the crisis of invention and have never themselves been submitted to the discipline of imitation. The result is that students who haven't had the time to construct an artistic culture of any kind are being tutored in the deconstructive suspicion proper to our time. I have seen one art school (not that long ago) where the first year course (what used to be the foundation course) had been transformed into a seminar in which the point was to "deconstruct" anything entering the classroom. One week it was an advertisement, another week it was the policy of this or that public art institution, and yet another week it was a student's work - a work done at home, that is, as if no assignment had been given to her beside the unspoken injunction to produce material to be deconstructed in the classroom. The ensuing paralysis was not just sad, it was revolting.

Of course, as I warned you at the beginning of my talk, I have simplified matters, and I have turned the world of present-day art schools into a caricature, just as I did with the old Academy and with the somewhat younger Bauhaus model. In the everyday reality of art schools things are a lot more complex, more subtle, more ambiguous. But since all of us, here, are gathered around the problematic and general issues of "perspectives in fine art education", I hope you understand that it is not on the level of our everyday endeavours that I have situated my remarks but on that of the historical ideological paradigms that we inherit from our institutions or with which, willy-nilly, we have to work. It is thus my contention, which I really want to offer as an open basis for discussion, that the triad of notions, "attitude-practice-deconstruction", is not the post-modern paradigm that supposedly substituted for the modern paradigm, "creativity-medium-invention". It is the same one, minus faith, plus suspicion. I tend to see it as a mere after-image, as the negative symptom of a historical transition whose positivity is not clear yet. As such it is quite interesting, and it can yield strong works of art. But for the teaching of art it is sterile. Once it is possible to put it down on paper, as I have just done, this means that its potential for negation has already become conventional (deconstruction is today's good taste), that its anguish is no longer of the kind that nourishes true artists (it is fake, because it is reconciled with the present); and that its suspicion is, unlike Descartes's doubt, not fruitful (it is aimed at the other and not at oneself).

I shall stop here, rather abruptly, on purpose. Having offered a diagnosis, I refuse to suggest a cure - which is not to say that the cure interests me less than the diagnosis. Quite the contrary. As some of you might know, I spent the past three years conceiving the project of a new art school on behalf of the City of Paris, until it was abandoned by the very same City of Paris for financial reasons. In the process I had dozens of meetings with artists, teachers, critics, intellectuals, technicians; I wrote a book on the issue of art schools, of which you have just heard the first fifteen pages; and I was lucky enough to be able to organise a one-month summer school for thirty-two students, as a sort of "dry-run" test of the future school, just before the project went down the drain. In the process I also learnt that there is no ready-made solution to the crisis in art schools; that the first thing to do was patiently to reconstitute a community of good artists who love art, who respect each other and their students, and who take their task as transmitters seriously; and that the last thing to do was to want to unite them around a banner, a programme or an ideology. I hope you will pardon me for refusing even to suggest that I might hold such a banner.

III

TINA's ACADEMY

Colin Cina

'TINA' is more accurately spelt T.I.N.A. (an acronym for "There Is No Alternative"). I begin with three personal anecdotes - illustrations of issues to be addressed in the main paper

Anecdote One: Who Is To Say Who? In the early spring of 1993 the Visual Arts department of the then Arts Council of Great Britain invited three heads of schools of fine art (I was one of them) to discuss the viability of schemes to offer art school technical facilities - workshop-processes, photo-labs and darkrooms, computers, printmaking presses and the like - as an accessible, cost-affordable resource for local or regional artists. We all agreed that this kind of access, in the evenings, weekends, during the summer vacation period, was too infrequently provided and set about to discuss how we might envisage arrangements that would help meet this palpable need and would also be seen to be legitimate and cost-controlled - if not indeed profitable - to the executive managers of the institutions that might become involved. At some point, late in the discussion, someone from our side asked: "How will we decide who is an artist and who is not an artist? People we do not know - who say they are local artists - may turn up at our schools asking for this scarcely available time to use our facilities. Perhaps we'll need some method for deciding their professional eligibility; otherwise we could frequently be excluding the artists we most want to assist". (Or words to that effect).

Commentary: There is not, after all, a national professional organisation or society, or academy, that has the state-recognised right to license visual artists to practise professionally. Neither is there any

41

existing U.K. organisation that might reveal the ambition to play that role and which the majority of the U.K. artist communities could be brought to acknowledge.

Anecdote Two: A Local Celebrity About ten years ago my wife was working for the social research unit of a national survey organisation. It had won a commission to appraise the initial results of the financially attractive early-retirement schemes that the Thatcher-led government had introduced in many areas of public service as part of their radical reforms: reductions in public bureaucracy to assist in rolling back the carpet of the State as their rhetoric put it. She was sent off to interview a man in his mid-fifties who had recently taken early retirement from a fairly senior local government post. He lived with his family in north-west London, quite close to the heathland parks of that area. His house was hung with small paintings and drawings, the majority of which appeared to be the work of one artist : well-crafted, traditionally rendered landscapes and genre scenes, most taken from picturesque spots in the locale, in a style somewhat closer to Constable than to Courbet. "Are these your paintings?" she asked, and he confirmed that they were. Not much later in the interview - which was essentially about how well he had adjusted to early retirement and about his future plans - the paintings re-appeared in their conversation. "You see, I am an artist now," he said. "I had been a self-taught amateur artist for years and now I can do it full time." "My husband's a professional painter," my wife remarked "but he also teaches in an art school, which takes up an awful lot of his time." "What kind of painter is he?" "Well...he works in a very different way from you. It's a very long time since he painted from landscape. He makes abstract works - very large canvases." "Has he had many exhibitions?" "Yes. He has a London gallery and of course he gets invited to be in group shows, sometimes overseas." "I'll bet he doesn't sell a lot of work, though?" "He sells works from time to time." "Yes, but is it enough to live on? ... Isn't that why he's teaching as well?" "Yes," she said, "that's true." "Well..." he said. "Let me explain why I asked you these questions: it will also provide what you need to put in your report of this interview. I took the early-retirement offer because I knew that I could make a financial success of being an artist. Without any disrespect to your husband and his fellow modernists, they are not the only artists in this country and I've good reason to believe that, on the whole, they are the least successful - in a national financial context, anyway. I enjoy making these little paintings and I can produce a fair number in a year. I show them in amateur art shows, professional landscape shows, occasionally the Royal Academy Summer Show, library exhibitions, small-town galleries - anywhere, in fact, where I can see an opportunity to sell. And I sell most of them; dozens of them each year. People enjoy owning them. I don't charge very much for them - a few hundred pounds, usually. But I'm making enough money to more than compensate for the difference between my salary and the pension. There are hundreds of artists like me - good craftsmen, traditionalists - hundreds...No one in his "artworld" ever remembers that we exist!"

Commentary: There are, indeed, two separate but overlapping "official" art communities in the U.K. The younger of the two is, of course, ourselves, i.e. those of us at this conference who can be described as the inheritors of modernism and its aftermath. We began by being dedicated to universalism and innovation, freeing ourselves - if we wished - from all historical ties and from "art as the appearance of truth", but in recent decades we have fractured into opposing factions and tendencies that live in a symbiotic form of visual debate, polarised between the extremes of Art made "for Art's sake" and art as cultural and political intervention. We work in a host of media and techniques, sometimes combining visual art media with other forms of cultural production. Nevertheless, the majority of us remain prepared to be categorised as painters, sculptors and the like, partly because we believe we are the sincere, occasionally subversive, inheritors of these disciplines and the particular, visual sensibilities that they represent, and partly because those who mediate for us in the art market enjoy the convenience of retaining these categories because they also infer a quasi-redemptive historical continuity with the celebrities of the pre-modernist periods.

We cannot accept that there is a definitive body of knowledge that informs and determines our practice and its manifold philosophical interpretations. Therefore our "modernity" differs fundamentally from that of those who work within scientifically constructed determinants because our kind of experimentation removes the need for objective verification and a priori constraints. Because we are thus unpredictable, esoteric and occasionally outrageous and yet often the inventors of art objects of transcendent, extraordinary beauty, we command a huge, if somehat bemused, public following and interest - verging upon the popular. Our pioneers certainly transformed public taste and, for better or worse, the visual environment (literally the"shape of 'things'") - despite our tendency to take a somewhat adversarial position towards utilitarianism.

In the decades since the Second World War we have come to control the substantial majority of institutions and organisations representing or premeditatedly shaping British visual culture. We have therefore enjoyed a variety of forms of state and public patronage but never sufficient to sustain the burgeoning community we have become. We dominate the vast majority of Britain's sixty or so art schools and also the majority of architecture schools; and we are networked nationally and internationally, supported by and mediated by a parallel critic, museum and dealer infrastructure that commands a significantly large amount of the international visual art economy. As the dominant form of visual art practice in contemporary society, and as the creators of the most elite cultural commodity within it, we are presumed to hold a major responsibilty for the quality and diversity of visual culture. In the hypothetically tolerant multi-cultural society we have helped to create this infers responsibility for cultural inclusions - for a plurality that immediately subverts or negates the idealist universality of our original modernist project and reveals the inherent Eurocentricity that pervades it[1]. While we seem capable of absorbing this crisis intellectually and of supporting artists who externalise it in new forms of visual-cultural production, we do not yet seem consistently capable of meeting the need for the institutionalised pluralism it demands of us.

The elder of the two U.K. art communities is very probably also the larger of the two; the more than vestigial remains of the classical and neo-classical "academy" and medievally derived guild traditions now combined with characteristic visual features of the precursors of modernism (e.g. Pre-Raphaelites, Impressionists, Symbolists) plus, very recently, some tolerance of formalist and expressionist abstract art and "Pop" art deriving from the middle generation of artists who were stars of the sixties. The scholarship and production of this group's (Royal) academy core is enclosed by a collective memory that is quintessentially Eurocentric, within a deterministic body of knowledge it believes is its inheritance and which might help to explain its willingness to include more superficially talented "copyists" and enthusiasts for vernacular forms: the limners and renderers, genre-scene painters, colourists, portrait artists, trompe- l'oeil muralists, traditionally convinced amateurs. Their definitive "modernity" corresponds to the earliest idea of that category, i.e. original statements, if not innovation, which can be clearly connected to an earlier tradition if not to antiquity. Their principal institutions and mediators are the Royal Academy and its satellite regional academies, the Royal Scottish Aacdemy, the Royal West of England Academy and the Royal Society of Arts plus numerous other "Royal" art and craft societies, which give them as a grouping a more distinct, seemingly "state-approved" professional identity than their likely equivalents in many other Western European countries have. They have no powerful critical support nationally or internationally but they have immense local and regional critical support and a related dealer and exhibition network. As the anecdote infers, they are more often than not commercially and economically viable. There is popular demand for their work at all levels of society. Their attitude still influences one or two of the official art schools, a significant minority of architecture practices, the bulk of adult-education art classes and a host of small, private art colleges. They may well believe that they are a kind of art-practice equivalent of the "silent majority". They are certainly an important characteristic of British visual culture as it is actually experienced by our citizens.

Anecdote Three: Mediocrity Licensed as Competence Again, about a year ago, I was invited to a meeting of the Arts and Entertainment Training Board, an organisation sponsored by the Department of

Employment and a key element in the current development of NVQs (National Vocational Qualifications). These constitute a new training and assessment system for the U.K. workforce based on sets and levels of predetermined "competences" and objectified skills that, once in appositely defined form, will be progressively applied to almost any craft, job-skill or profession. They represent a training-based approach to employability skills, which this government perceives to be necessary to the survival and effectiveness of the U.K.'s industry, service economy and societal needs. They are publicised as new forms of job-related education, to be a widely accessible means of "self-development" for employees sponsored by their employers but also generally available to adult U.K. citizens; and to guarantee basic standards of work skills within an employment sector - from plumbers to psychiatrists, from bricklayers to bio-chemists - through a network of training and assessment centres. (Yet another feature of the radical Right's approach to delivering a "competitive market economy".) The Arts and Entertainment Training Board has responsibility for consultations to enable the construction of relevant training requirements and assessment criteria for their sector of employment, e.g. actors, stage hands, film editors, museum technicians, piano tuners. This entails months of "field research" and consultative meetings leading to thousands of rules, assessment formats and guidelines being written down - task by task, craft by craft, skill by skill, profession by profession. "Artists" are an included category, with their own discrete set of training, competence and assessment criteria. Apparently we had been left out of the NVQ development for a long period and, indeed, had only been brought into the scheme because representative groups of artists had protested at their exclusion. A consultative "Fine Art" group, with delegates from various artists' societies and organisations, had been in session for months; a massive survey of artists had been commissioned to inform it. I, with about a dozen similarly experienced colleagues from further and higher art education, was consulted at the point when an almost complete draft set of "competences" and assessment criteria was seen to need some external exposure and debate.

Much of the initial levels of fine art training criteria and competence descriptions read in a fairly commonsense way, comprising the kinds of skills and technical or historical information you would expect beginners to learn at secondary school art classes, on Foundation courses, possibly even in the early phases of a fine art degree course. When it came on to the higher professional territories - when it attempted to describe competences for self-expressive powers, creativity, critical awareness - the draft was being very brave, very contemporaneous, in its breadth of definitions of the art practices it sought to apply these competences to. But many of us there that day felt it was somewhat over-optimistic, if not naïve, in its assumptions of how such fluid and inter-related attributes of artistic capability were to be fairly and relevantly assessed in their application within a diversity of practice, ranging from craft-based or academic painting, carving and modelling through to conceptually derived performance art, image-text art, installation art. There was even a set of criteria for "anti-art". And given the open, public-access characteristics of the scheme, we were back to the question of "Who, to begin with, and who, in the end, will believe they are empowered to decide who the artists are?"

Commentary: The long-term effects of the Romantic movement - the notion of the "single genius", the self-imposed artistic isolation characteristic of our epoch and the resultant rupture of academy-led artist communities in Western Europe - put paid to national organisations of professional artists decades before modernist theory and practice became dominant. We have no effective equivalent of the R.I.B.A., The Royal College of Surgeons or of Nursing, The Musicians Union, The Society for Industrial Artists and Designers, The Institute of Chartered Surveyors or of Accountants, and the like: institutions that have, indeed, played an important role in negotiating an NVQ structure for their professions and which would retain the power to bestow or withhold a professional licence to practise once NVQs are available.

As we 20th-century British artists have chosen to celebrate our professional "chaos" rather than to retain the protective institutional boundaries provided by the "classic" academies, these proposed new fine art competence qualifications seemed potentially likely, to me at least, to open doors to a form of regulation of art practice, the like of which had not been seen since the hegemony of the medieval guilds.

Sitting there at the consultative meeting, I remembered Lunacharsky and his Soviet examining committees. It was as if his ghost was standing by my shoulder, whispering: "You see, we had the right idea all along . . . Maybe we were a little too metaphysical in our approach, then . . . all that stuff from Lenin about artists having skills dedicated to a political and social mission. Well, maybe it was the wrong political ideology, anyway, in which to test the idea of artistic deviation . . . But these NVQ assessments invented by your petite bourgeoisie are exactly how we should have done it. I tell you, they'll be erecting statues to me all over Britain in the years to come. I feel I am the true pioneer of NVQs!"

But that is not the only point of this third anecdote. The day had begun with descriptions and explanations of the generic principles of the scheme, which is based upon four levels of assessed competences. You might say that the lad carrying the bricks for the bricklayer, the hod-carrier, has to achieve Level 1 competences; the bricklayer has to achieve Level 2; his employer's architect's draughtsman has to achieve Level 3 and the architect is Level 4. Is that the case? we asked. Are the graduate professions, architects, surgeons, physicists, film directors, economists, Level 4? The man from the Ministry thought for a while and replied that this was not necessarily the case; the higher Levels were not to be understood as a specific reflection of graduate or postgraduate achievement. It would only be Level 4 if their professional responsibilities included "management" responsibility. Otherwise, they would be assessed at the top of Level 3. Game, set and match to the petite bourgeoisie! Well, perhaps.

My three anecdotes serve to begin to illustrate the social fragility of contemporary British fine art education institutions in comparison with the confident certainties of the academy and guild traditions that they replaced. Each anecdote is intended to suggest an attendant reality, that, alongside our schools and the artists we help develop, there remains an older, often anachronistic, apparatus for visual art production that, at the very least, can claim direct lineage with the proud craftsmanship of Old Europe while remaining demonstrably popular in both mass-consumer culture and within the high Establishment. It provides justification to those who seek to make fine art education more utilitarian, those impressed by the neo-conservative's call that simplifying, futile change must be given priority because sound economic management insists that "There Is No Alternative". Perhaps innocently, unintentionally, it promotes the opportunity to dilute and generalise fine art education.

The complex esoteric learning strategies that characterise the internal dynamics of the advanced contemporary specialist fine art school - the convergence of disciplines, the overt experimentalism, the dedication to innovation and the ever-shifting, if still limited, pluralism - are tolerated by our institutional managers and politicians, I would argue, only because these academic imperatives of specialist fine art education are externally acknowledged as expedient prerequisites for successful replenishment of an elite, yet debased and commodified, "modern art" market. Alongside music conservatoires and film schools, specialist fine art courses join the hot-house culture of the arts education "market garden".

This vulnerability prevails because the deeper relevance of the pedagogy of contemporary fine art schools, which has momentarily regained the capacity both to reflect upon and to reform a plurality of contemporary practice, is still too new - not yet as firmly rooted in European cultural understanding as the previous academic methods surely were. The educational mission of our "anti-academy" must be recognisably more than prototypical of a "universalism" that has long ago lost touch with its idealist, utopian dream.

The "inclusions", the deeper level of socio-cultural integration that we art-educator-artists so crucially need to achieve for our programme is dependent upon our willingness and our ability to relocate our schools **within** their communities rather than remain **above** the local actualities of "Europe". We must become capable of anticipating, debating and tangibly affecting the social, political and demographic contexts that will bear upon the new, "open", yet inherently nationalistic Europe that the collective Western body politic seems impelled to create. As artists, we may well achieve this emblematically through visual rather than verbal and instrumental deeds - as did Courbet or Beuys. But to believe, as the ascendant politics would have us believe, that we will achieve anything of lasting relevance as educators by simplistically and opportunistically addressing this new Europe as an Art Market among art markets would be an abdication of our responsibilities to our students and to the diverse regional crises that so many of their home communities experience.

Now, I admit that I am condensing this description but we artists know the power of iconic simplification. This TINA Academy - this market-led, diluted model - is indeed emblematic of the opportunistic controls that have recently but increasingly manifested themselves in our universities, academies and schools. There are few natural allies to turn to in our consternation at the simplistic bureaucratisation and mercantilism now so frequently demanded as a condition of institutional autonomy.

The politically ascendant group asserts that such autonomy will be as finite as our capability to survive in an education "market". We cannot continue to elude this by relying upon "special pleading" for protection from those Establishment figures who might mediate for us, justified by a presumed - yet historically fragile - relationship of contemporary fine art education to national cultural heritage or by its potential to foster innovative cultural production that will contribute to economic well-being (a more provable case, in fact). The political forces we contend with acknowledge both of these attributes while continuing to demand radical reorganisation in the interests of market efficiency.

The principle, that we know and protect as "academic freedom"; the potential for the academically licensed scholar within both the academy and the university to dissent against or criticise accepted principle as freely as he or she chooses and an essential element of the intellect-at-play factor within any scholarly colloquium: at least this tolerance remains. Given the tendency to paranoia in the contemporary political climate, academic freedom might only survive in compromised form as part of an unspoken compact between the academic institution and the State, reflecting an expedient methodology for generating intellectual innovation within the walls of the academy rather than being seen to flourish openly as the democratic prerogative it was intended to be.

The idea of "academy" began in Florence during the early Renaissance to describe informal discursive gatherings of clerics and scholars, precipitated by the literary and scientific curiosity inherent in an emerging humanist philosophy. The proliferation of academies as formally regulated national institutions was a later, 16th-to-17th-century, European invention[2]; to our eyes a more arcane adaptation of the original idea, established to be at the service of emperors, kings and dukes. They were re-created in this more complex form (sandwiched between an already established hierarchy of universities on one side and guilds on the other) so as to guarantee imperial possession of specialised, albeit esoteric, knowledge and skills via focused (therefore controlled) patronage of the scholars within their walls - an arrangement that, to an extent, remains to this day. Although specialised on a discipline, they were thus premeditatedly different in form, intention and constitution from the craft and professional guilds that had dominated European socio-economic, and therefore cultural, organisation since early medieval times and which remained in place until the 19th century.

The historical record suggests that many academies, like the guilds, were eventually more likely than not to decelerate the pace of innovation in their field - through a tendency to conservatism and jealous protection of the "ownership" of their discipline/s and through complex rule-making. Nevertheless, their internal organisation, deriving from their original, more social Florentine prototype, often remained modelled upon a pragmatic, if nostalgic, interpretation of the Graeco-Platonic intellectual forum, the original gatherings in the grove of Akademe: i.e. they were/are inherently colloquial and in a particular adult sense "playful" within their licensed range of operations. Within this primary organisational logic, a circle of scholar-practitioners, sharing a body of knowledge, is led by an elected leader.

The Academy of Art, again originating informally in the Florence of the Medicis, follows a relatively similar development within a European-wide system that eventually came to serve 17th- century state absolutism and mercantilism simultaneously[3] but with the significant difference that these early art academies more immediately became associated with "education" - the education of the aspiring artist. Italian Renaissance secularisation of cultural production led, as we know, to an elevated repositioning of the artist within European society and to the rapid emergence of aesthetic connoisseurship within its culture. "Art" needed to become separated from "Craft" and leading artists sought to detach themselves from the guild mentality; "the painter was to be taught knowledge more than skill" was how Leonardo summarised the argument. Such early anticipation of autonomous art defined as a discrete form of knowledge and experimentation led to argument for the abandonment of training methods for student artists that were based exclusively on apprenticeship; or for the need to augment them, if not replace, with a visual, humanist education involving both practical and theoretical studies. The "monotechnic" potential of a maturing academy system appeared to lend itself easily to such radical change in the nature and intention of art education - albeit still then dedicated to the service of the empire, church and state.

The historical archive suggests that while Leonardo da Vinci probably began this debate at the start of the 16th century - i.e. shortly before his death - it was Vasari, in 1562, who crystallised his altruistic idea of art education within the first formally successful proposal for a state-sponsored art academy, the Accademia del Disegno. He envisaged this as an institution that would serve as a forum for the artist elite of the period, as their representative voice in matters of contract and professional probity - and, as it turned out, somewhat more haphazardly, as a school based upon Leonardo's aforementioned principles. The die was nevertheless cast. Across late 16th-century and 17th-century Europe first Mannerist, then Baroque, teaching academies of art proliferated, soon abandoning the Italian variants on the Vasari model for more and more prescriptive, complex and pedantic structures - dominated first by French then by German exemplars.

The fact that so many of these institutions and their imitations were able to survive the seismic shifts in philosophical, political and cultural practice that affected Europe over that 350-year period to the middle of this century is too time-consuming and diversionary to discuss here in detail: it is sufficient to remind ourselves that they did and without much alteration to their assumed academic objectives in the name of art, namely the study of the Antique and the Renaissance periods through copyist drawing. Indeed, some of these art education anachronisms persist in pockets and corners of every European state, with the very same rhetoric from both politician and academician supporting claims to their strategic role to protect national visual heritage and classically derived aesthetic values.

The transformation of art and design education that first emerged from mid 19th-century nation-state competition; from critique of design quality, or the absence of it, in mass-produced goods; then from the subsequent influence of the Arts and Crafts Movement in Britain and its counterparts in mainland Europe; and particularly from the myriad of "anti-academic" art and architecture movements that captured the collective European imagination. All of these progenitors of the modernist period precipitated radical change in the nature and accessibility of the state or city art academy in a rapidly developing mass-consumer culture and laid the ground for the institutions we know and need to discuss today.

Despite the fact that the prototypical 20th-century art school quickly jettisoned almost all of the arcane, anachronistic, pedagogical baggage that the academy tradition brought with it, there was one significant aspect of academic organisation that, with the complicit approval of their state or city sponsors, and in tandem with universities, they rightly did not abandon. I refer to centuries of continuity of belief in the need for academic communities to be headed by master practitioners, genuine professors of the subject - at the very least by leading academics in the discipline of the school.

This supposition of needing to be led, or I should now say "managed", by one of their own is a sensitive issue that bears upon almost any group of specialised professionals working in the contemporary corporate or state organisation. It has its roots in the original idea of academy organisation but it is even more understandable when examined at deeper levels of the characteristics of professional groups within an organisation. The distinct identities of specialised professional communities[4] are founded upon shared experience of study and purposeful practice of their subject; upon shared values and ethics; upon a consensual understanding of the role that they play in society; and upon a common - probably esoteric -"technical language". As we noted earlier, many such groups are licensed to practice by their own state-recognised, professional body or have powerful professionally led agencies to lobby on their behalf.

So, while the active professional artist working in education needs to recognise and respect the particular service to his/her school that this additional vocation demands, it must surely be a **subsidiary** organisational loyalty. The primary allegiance tends to remain to their professional discipline and its external agencies and histories, which somehow once combined to motivate his or her "life-chance": determining the skills required, and hence the self-fulfilling achievements, hence the professional credibility to earn a living - even if partially through teaching.

The strategy of appointing or electing[5] an accomplished art practitioner or a respected scholar as executive leader removes the tension between a school's instrumental need for the specialised expertise that is provided by a cosmopolitan group of artists and theorists and the school's reasonable expectation of their organisational loyalty.

This single-leadership aspect of the academy model was a strategic imperative as much for the ascendant modernist artists, architects and designers who radically reformed the 20th-century art school as it had been for the art-academicians whose role they usurped - enabling an entirely different concept of art education to emerge within historically familiar organisational circumstances. The professional artist as leader-administrator can be tyrant or altruistic saint in this story (usually somewhere in between). It is their external communication skills, their ambassadorial capability on behalf of their school, welded to a commitment to the source discipline and their specialised knowledge of it, which enable their academic communities to function confidently. Suffice it now to remind you that the majority of European art schools remain dedicatedly organised in this way. A growing minority (regrettably, a significant number within the U.K.) now find themselves required to operate within a very different set of "managerial" strategies, irrespective of their internal realities.

What we need to examine at this point is the difference between the contemporary bureaucratic/managerial perspective of state-institutionalised art education and that of its professional artist-teachers - a difference that I believe is gradually but definitely creating a dysfunctional academic environment within British art education. The only common ground between the two might be a belief in maintaining "quality" - but even then, in the context of the relatively esoteric processes of contemporary fine art education, the means to judge this would be likely to emerge from entirely different value constructs.

You will surely recognise that I am beginning to probe at a set of issues, too little discussed in our forum, that progressively encroach upon the everyday experience of the artist-teacher and his or her students. For who in the U.K. can deny that we now work in a broad political/institutional milieu that has become obsessed with the quasi-science of "quality control"; which has convinced itself that the methods and abstractions of "scientific-management" theory and its partner "accountability" are a more effective process of organising the provision of education than is reliance upon the percipience of dedicated academic community leadership that is supported by skilled administration?

Within the "classic" management theory[6] employees are assumed to be working primarily to gain a living wage; therefore their passivity wedded to expedient company loyalty is a built-in supposition of such management strategy. The employee's likelihood to make mistakes is an anticipated "performance" problem to be "managed" by those higher in the hierarchy who are responsible for controlling "quality". In applying such theory to newly autonomous higher education institutions, the Academic Leader-Administrator approach has to be replaced by the Executive Manager approach.

The reforming neo-Conservative policies that have swept over U.K. higher education since the middle 1980s brought a management and marketing obsession with them. It seems to be the inevitable by-product of all current governmental perceptions of how to make two of society's vital services, health care and education, more "efficient". As with hospitals, schools and colleges are given institutional and financial autonomy and corporate company status, severed from the city or regional authorities who were previously able to provide bureaucratic and technical maintenance services that we now have to redevelop for ourselves. It was a tempting alternative to the evident constraints of the previous arrangements, until we were told to operate "as a market" in "market conditions" - that our students were "clients", that managers must be "allowed to manage". We are therefore counselled, if not coerced, to provide ourselves with management expertise that can objectively interpret and organise this new world we find ourselves in. This we cannot do to ourselves without destroying our professional and academic credibility, and our political masters know this. Thus, for us to be organisationally - and therefore politically - secure, the genuinely professional "manager of managers" must needs arrive or self-mutate within our institutions. Just like us, they have refined specialist skills and their professional allegiance is to their (new) discipline and to its external agencies and histories.

In the revised institutional model that I have seen so often in the U.K. these past five years, skilled academic leaders originally appointed for their nationally or internationally recognised status as artists and teachers may be corralled in middle-management roles while being exhorted to adopt business-like methods. Wholesome academic communities with once-distinct identities may be reorganised as tuition factories - "generalised", "unitised" and "modularised" in the interests of parsimony masquerading as increased "choice" for students. I cannot deny being grateful that the large corporate institution I work within has steadfastly refused to take this path. No one seems to notice that the longer-established North American modularity models, from which this course-structure approach is borrowed, are an evident failure, quietly being abandoned by their institutions.

I admit to speaking about this experience from the viewpoint of a fine art educator who has somehow managed to survive in these circumstances without experiencing such virtually terminal levels of damage to the small academic community and the courses for which I have responsibility. But the irony of this is the probability that the reason for my school's survival as a truly specialist area of fine art studies emanates not from the strength of resistance to "modularity" and the like (as some of my colleagues would like to suppose) but from a management and government recognition of the prestige (which translates into marketable value) of some few metropolitan courses as "specialist centres of excellence". A minority of schools like mine can be tolerated within the reformed national provision because we seem capable of being highly appreciated, sought after and even on occasion profitable by being allowed to remain much as we were originally intended - and therefore different from so many of our local and regional fine art schools, now required to have a generality and utility of purpose in order to serve mass needs.

It is difficult to find much useful research that has studied the very particular operational constructions that have succeded in surviving and thriving within contemporary specialist fine art education. This is all too clearly a pressing imperative, given the uniformity of approach to reviewing or "auditing" the locally asserted quality of higher education that has been developed very recently in the U.K. and which must also apply to specialist fine art courses. Once again, a distinctly managerial analysis of components and requirements dominates the approach to auditing the course experience *per se*. Inherent in this is the quality controller's assumption (possibly a sincere attempt to forestall inadequate planning of a curriculum and syllabus) that all components of courses, all of the organisational arrangements for the student-learner, need to be defined as precisely and chronologically as possible; that any indications of randomness in, for example, the deployment of teaching resources displays innefficiency, poor academic management, possibly even lax financial controls. The same attitude applies to scrutiny of aims and progression within a course. Again, it is assumed that pedagogic intention is deterministically linked to a previsioned progression of particular learning experiences and their intended outcomes - that all of this must be made clear, in advance, to the initiate student. It may well be that this kind of approach still has its place in some faculties within the higher education sector but for fine art education this is a late 20th-century redemption of guild and academy teaching methods.

My experience of devising and providing advanced-level fine art education, dedicated to enabling student-artists to become informed, self-organised and creatively capable of practising professionally suggests that an almost opposite, although equally painstaking, approach is the more relevant, more successful and decidedly more "cost-beneficial" - by virtually reversing these somewhat bureaucratic perceptions of academic organisation.

Specialist fine art education that is pro-actively aware of the fluid external conditions for art practice has learnt to operate within a responsive yet comparatively minimal organisational specification so as to give a student maximum capacity for self-organised learning - given its belief that there is no longer an approved or definitive body of knowledge or range of skills within which the learning trajectory can be precisely predetermined. While the teaching staff - the artist-teachers, theorists and historians - may seem, for line management purposes, to be defined as a hierarchy - course leaders, principal lecturers, lecturers, visiting teachers etc. - they function most effectively as a matrix of facilitating, enabling, orchestrating resources to support a critique-led environment and to elucidate tangibly the plurality of art practice, which, ideally, they should also represent by their own creative practice.

Within these frameworks for experience the student will learn to learn very effectively. What the bureaucratic mind might perceive to be a worrisome randomness is, in fact, maximised flexibility within an integrated organic, teaching strategy.

In these conditions the rate of development during the course will be more variable from student-artist to student-artist than it would be within a structured programme. Yet this variability is entirely concomitant with the reality of a professional artist's experience of working life; student peer-group appreciation of it becomes an important element of their emerging professional awareness and capability. The methodology for assessment also has to be in empathy with this likelihood of varying development. This is not a problem: it simply removes to a very significant extent the need to predetermine quotas and quantities of anticipated achievement within the required assessment criteria. The logical consequence of this approach is that a tutor-imposed application of progressively more difficult tasks, projects or bodies of information within the duration of a fine art course of this type recedes in strategic importance. Instead it offers students access to all information and technical resources and creates student responsibility to set his/her own level of enquiry, research and resolution, while the school provides artists-as-teachers who are capable of recognising when a fine art student needs to be criticised or encouraged and primed with information and when to be left alone. Regular, discursive reviews - of work achieved or of work in progress - and collective participation in debating the resultant artworks become the major stabilisers of this methodology, which, in its successfully delivered entirety, is very demanding of commitment and self-management from the students and work-intensive for the staff but very satisfying for the fine art academic communities who experience it. It is also, unfortunately, very difficult to describe to the managerial mind, particularly if that mind has little awareness of the actual demands and diversity of late 20th-century practice in art.

The operational, philosophical and ethical problems that confront a fine art school trapped within the overly managerial environment that currently controls so much of the former polytechnic sector of U.K. higher education need to be addressed publicly. The tendency in Britain today to keep debates about the purpose and content of advanced fine art education separate from the implications of its enclosure within the radically altered institutions in which the majority of fine art degree courses must live is short-sighted and politically naïve. Some optimists suppose that a change of government will sweep away these mechanistic tendencies in fine art education reforms. There is little evidence to suggest that this would be the case. There is rather too much evidence accruing that suggests that, hearing no clear voices of dissent, the Ministries of Education and Culture of a recession-bound European mainland are likely to seize expediently upon many of the negative tenets of these new U.K. Academies of "No Alternative".

NOTES

1   "This redefinition of the creative subject as a multiple, complex process is also an attempt to avoid relativism and to rethink the unity of the subject, without reference to humanistic beliefs, without dualistic oppositions, linking instead body and mind in a new flux of self.

In other words, in my view, there cannot be lasting social change or meaningful contemporary creativity without the construction of new kinds of kinds of desiring subjects as molecular, nomadic and multiple. I take it as the task of the artists, as well as of other critical intellectuals, to have the courage to face complexity, differences, and the absolute loss of monolithic schemes of thought. For as the American artist Martha Rozler put it: 'There cannot be fragments where there is no whole.' " Rosi Braidotti, conclusion of **United States of Europe or United Colours of Benetton?** in **Differences 2** (No. 3)

2 For detailed reference material on this development see N. Pevsner, **Academies of Art** (Cambridge University Press, 1940)

3 The early academies often contained students (who would also, where appropriate, continue with their guild apprenticeships) and the historical record shows that some soon developed wholly into educational institutions or developed a programmatic teaching sub-role but they were not, despite this observation, generically intended to be synonymous with the concept of the School. The long-established academy that has become primarily school-like has mutated out of its originators' intended function - however worthy an institution it may have become.

The eventual intellectual autonomy of the academy from the 17th century onwards - through the gradual retraction of clerical opposition to experimentation, the victorious bourgeois revolutions and the historic period of European Enlightenment on to the Industrial Revolution was a false, or, at least, a partial freedom. The political apparatus of the constitutional monarchies and, eventually, the democratic, quasi-secular states that emerged soon reasserted that same control of academic patronage for reasons of political/economic expediency if not for full-blown ideological necessity. The major national and city academies survived these waves of renegotiation of their place within the European Establishment, and until very recently (albeit with certain totalitarian exceptions) the internal workings of the European academy was left relatively untouched when compared with almost any other institution of the state - thus enabling the prescriptive form and content of their schools, and particularly in what we would now call "creative and performing arts education", forcefully to influence the syllabuses of all levels of schools provision until the end of the 19th century.

4 See Meredydd Hughes, **Leadership In Professionally Staffed Organisations** in Hughes, Ribbins and Thomas **Managing Education** (Holt, Rinehart and Winston, London, 1985)

5 *Ibid.*

6   Deriving from what has come to be known as Taylorism - an early
20th-century theory of management and control of industrial
workforces, which, in turn, was based upon the command
structure of the reformed Prussian Army of Frederick the Great -
this "classic" management approach is predicated on the
assumption that individual workers who fulfil tasks low in the
hierarchical order of the organisation need not know too much
about the overall intention of the production process and its
outcome, while it demands their commitment to maximised
"quality" production as a prime indicator of their loyalty and
efficiency. He or she might know that they are making part of a
refrigerator or a hamburger or a guided missile. . . .or an artist;
they are not, as task workers "on the line", expected to need much
information as to mechanical or design principle, investment
strategy, profit margin, marketing guarantees or the safety of the
product to engender this commitment in themselves - even if they
might gain access to such information on their
company/organisation through the media available to them as
"free" citizens.

See also Gareth Morgan, **The Trap of Favoured Ways of
Thinking** (p. 201) and **Organisation As Flux and Transformation**
(p. 238), **in Images of Organisation** (Sage, Beverley Hills, 1986)

IV

WHY CRITICAL REGIONALISM TODAY?

Alexander Tzonis and Liane Lefaivre

In the past ten years, since the term was introduced,[1] critical regionalism has emerged as one of the alternatives to a clearly ageing post-Modernism and to post-Modernism's younger but prematurely ailing sibling, deconstruction. Yet for many people, even for those who believe that post-Modernism is waning and that deconstruction is no substitute for it, the meaning and appropriateness of regionalism is questionable. How can one be regionalist in a world that is increasingly becoming one global economically and technologically interdependent whole; where universal mobility is taking architects and users of architecture across borders and through continents at an unprecedented speed? More pointedly, how can one be regionalist today when regions in the cultural, political and social sense, based on the idea of ethnic identity, are disintegrating before our eyes? It sounds like a contradiction in terms.

No building today is capable of arousing feelings like those that the Cathedral of Strasbourg aroused in the heart of the first Romantic regionalist, the young Goethe, in 1772 that sense of individual and local architectural values symbolising an aspiration for emancipation from universal alien design canons, a sense of belonging to a single racial community. No building can talk to the viewer directly and immediately "without the aid of a translator" as it did to him, and make the viewer rush to embrace it as Goethe wanted to embrace the cathedral.[2] Nor can contemporary buildings possess, as buildings possessed for John Ruskin, a mid 19th-century Romantic regionalist, that strong quality of "sympathy", "affinity", "memory" and "familiarity", a "deep sense of voicefulness" that convincingly speaks of the past as if it were one with the present, telling us "all we need to know of national feeling or achievement". Even less can a building still evoke that same sense of revolt and righteousness. To look again to the topography of the region as a source of inspiration - as Viollet-le-Duc did when he took Mont-Blanc as an archetypal image, a paradigmatic building on which to base his design for his one building, La Vedette[3] can only be an exercise in anachronism today. Still less can one go back to cultivating the *genius loci* in the manner of the early 18th-century Picturesque Regionalists[4] those "brave Britons" who in the words of Alexander Pope used local elements as a means of manifesting their desire for emancipation from "despised" "foreign laws" and the "formal Mockery" of the absolutist classical order.

Surely Proust, whose very different ideas about the mechanisms of familiarisation and memory evolved out of an early apprenticeship to Ruskin[5], was right. **Swann's Way** (1913), the first volume of **A la recherche du temps perdu**, finishes with the hero reflecting sadly on the houses and avenues of Combray and of the Paris of his youth that are now "all fugitive", mere memories, irretrievable things of the past. "The reality I have known no longer exists," he sighs. This is the sigh of a culturally, politically, ethnically, sexually ambivalent "cosmopolitan" intellectual, but it is also the sign of a civilisation that has lost identifiable regions, collective social structures and the collective representations that went with them, a syndrome of the tragic realisation that community and place cannot be recaptured.

Given this loss of region, how is it possible for regionalist architecture to be anything more than, at best, a sentimental cosy indulgence in nostalgia for a bygone era, having nothing to do with Proust's art and everything to do with what we have called Proust's syndrome, citing highly typified regional fragments and gluing them together in a fake, a pastiche, kitsch, good only for commercial facilities, restaurants, hotels, and other emporia; or, at worst, a form of atavism, a setting for a xenophobic, neo-tribal racist hallucination? How is it possible for such a regionalist architecture, whether libertarian or totalitarian, commercial or propagandistic, in its "as-if" overfamiliarity, to be anything but a kind of architectural pornography?

We would like to argue that one contemporary trend of regionalist architecture - critical regionalism - is a more original movement that has come about as a response to new problems posed by contemporary global development, of which it is strongly critical, and that the poetics of this new movement are to a great extent different from yet not antithetical to other architectural regionalist techniques of the past. In fact the beginning of this new kind of regionalism coincided with the realisation of the obsolescence of traditional perceptions of regions as static closed entities corresponding to similarly invariant, insular groups, and the outworn character of traditional regionalist architectural modes of expression. These realisations have mounted as universal culture, economy and technology have expanded, and as regions have melted and fused into capitals, capitals into metropolises, metropolises into Patrick Geddes's "conurbations"[6] and Jean Gottmann's "megalopolises"[7] and these in turn into Melvin Webber's ultimate post-industrial "world realms".[8]

This new trend of regionalism is not only a defence against the obsolescence of the region itself but also a reaction to a perverse totalitarian *Heimatsarchitektur* regionalism that spread during the decade before the Second World War. It is clear that from its earliest inception this new regionalism shared with the entire tradition of regionalism since its earliest inception - Romantic regionalism and Picturesque regionalism - a commitment to "placeness" and a use of regional design elements as a means of confronting a universalist order of architecture that is seen as dominating or oppressive. But it also contains a new idea, one that is essential to critical regionalism: that of "place" with a meaning that goes beyond ethnicity, not to mention against the grain of nationalist insularity. Much of this discussion is to be found first in the writings of Lewis Mumford.

In his **The South in Architecture**[9] Mumford evoked the architecture of H. H. Richardson as an example of regionalism in architecture. The book is not without an element of dramatising simplicity in its account of certain complex historical phenomena, but its importance lies in Mumford's interpretation of Richardson's architecture, largely unknown at that time. Regionalist Mumford praises his buildings for the critical confrontation and alternative they offer to the "despotic" Beaux-Arts architecture that Mumford links en masse to the imperial "exploitation and colonisation and conquest of Asia, Africa and the Americas" as well as to what had been during Richardson's time. The East Coast banking Establishment, which in its architectural expression had "placed a premium upon the façade". Mumford praised Richardson for his refusal "to place the premium upon the façade" and for carrying out through regionalism the "social task of architecture".

In addition Mumford opposed Richardson's regionalism to the totalitarian type of regionalism that was being propounded in Nazi Germany at the time. He shows that an architecture can provide an identity and express the specifics of a programme without the "deification of *Heimatsarchitektur*", the "cult of the relics of another imperial age" and a neo-tribal creation of a "deep unbridgeable gulf between the peoples of the earth". Mumford put forth a concept of regionalism that upheld, on the contrary, the idea of a common humanity, explicitly free of racial or tribal or ethnic dimensions. Last but not least Mumford used the example of Richardson to juxtapose regionalism polemically with another kind of "despotism", that of the "mechanical order" and of the "absurdities" of a mindless use of technology.

After the war Mumford did not return to the attack on *Heimat*. His regionalist position focused on the developing post-war International Style, which he felt had deviated from the original objectives of the modern movement in architecture and succumbed to the very forces it was created to reform. He reacted against an architecture of false modernity that emulated modernity through the rote repetition of surface effects where once more "the premium is placed upon the façade". Thus the International Style replaced Beaux-Arts as the target of Mumford's criticism.

In 1947, in his famous column "Skyline" in the **New Yorker**[10], the tone was provocative and polemical, almost pugnacious. Referring to Henry Russell Hitchcock's turn to "personalism" and Siegfried Giedion's new enthusiasm for "the monumental and the symbolic", he complained that modern architecture was being subverted from within by critics who had been closely identified with the modern movement's preoccupation with objectivity and plain reality. As a critical confrontation to what he saw as a debased post-war "modernism," he proposed the so-called Bay Region Style of California of William Wurster and his associates, calling it a "native and humane form of modernism", which as a "product of the meeting of Oriental and Occidental traditions" was "far more truly a universal style than the international style of the 1930s", because it "permits **regional** adaptations".

The article created an enormous stir, which led to an open debate at the Museum of Modern Art on the evening of 11th February 1948. The title, **What is happening to Modern Architecture?**, reflecteed the concerns of the organisers.[11] The speakers included some of the main figures of post-war modernism: Alfred Barr Jr.(Director of the Museum), Henry Russell Hitchcock, Philip Johnson, Walter Gropius, Marcel Breuer, Serge Chermayeff and George Nelson, and Mumford himself.

Most of the participants completely missed Mumford's redefinition of regionalism. In spite of Mumford's insistence that it was "a sample of internationalism, not a sample of localism and limited effort"[12], Alfred Barr referred to it dismissively as the *Neue Gemütlichkeit*, the International Cottage Style; as for Gropius, he read into it "a chauvinistic sentimental national prejudice". The one exception was Hitchcock. He was sensitive to the real critical impact of the notion. "Criticism - for it is criticism - that is implicit" in Mumford's article was, according to Hitchcock, "a criticism of the International Style conceived in the limited sense..." But then he commented that "this criticism and the steps that have been taken are to be subsumed in a more general problem", which in his familiar formalist way he identified as "the problem of expression in architecture".[13]

Mumford's ideas were read, praised and dutifully ignored. Or they were subverted, as in the case of the "regionalist" epidermic concrete-lace-screened facades of such new projects, at that time widely publicised, as Edward Durell Stone's Pakistan Institute of Science and Technology, Walter Gropius's University of Baghdad and Yamasaki's entry for the United States Embassy in London. While these efforts to restore the "imperial façade" were being deployed, technocracy, bureaucracy and real estate had their equally imperial way, with as sole result widespread anomie and atrophy.

It was in Europe that the new approach to regionalism was used for a critical confrontation with the state of architecture after the Second World War, although the word "regionalism" was rarely used. It emerged a few years after Mumford's polemic at the MOMA. In at least one sense the Europeans developed the Mumford thesis further, in the "architecturalness" with which they carried out their analysis and their ability to implement these ideas in concrete projects of often considerable scale.

In an article entitled **Regionalism and Modern Architecture**[14] the young James Stirling juxtaposed regionalism to what he called "the so-called International Style combined with a strong dose of monumental eclectic neo-historicism" that was dominant, and promoted the "new traditionalism" that took into account local technological and economic realities. Furthermore, he designed projects for his Village Project (1955) and his Preston Infill Housing (1957-9), which in their respective incorporation of regional and working-class neighbourhood elements constituted a strong implicit critique of the post-war New Monumentality.[15]

A number of other interesting regionalist projects on the same lines were designed in England by the "new empiricists", whose regionalist outlook was influenced by Scandinavian architecture or by Aalto. The issue of regionalism was also discussed by Team X as a critique of New

Monumentality and found its way into several of its projects, especially the early work of Candilis, Josic and Woods in North Africa. Also critical of the neo-formalist and technocratic architecture of the International Style of the 1950s were many Italian practitioners and theoreticians: the architects of INA-Casa, especially Giancarlo de Carlo in his shops and apartment buildings in Matera; and Ernesto Rogers, both as editorialist at **Casabella** and as designer of the Torre Velasca (1958) in Milan.

The Torre Velasca was widely covered by the press internationally and its regionalist expression as a critique of International Style was acknowledged. Gerhard Kallmann wrote one of the most penetrating reviews in **Architectural Forum** in February 1958. He saw it as "a valiant essay in the neglected art of fitting modern architecture into a historic continuity of building" while avoiding "folkloristic revivalism" and "sentimental eclecticism". Rogers himself in his own article for **Casabella** on **Our Responsibility toward Tradition** (August 1954) attacked the dogmatism of those modernists who "fail to realise that the modern style contrasts with the old precisely because it laid the ground for a dynamic approach to problems" as well as of "neo-arcadian populism", which was "anachronistic if not hypocritical or downright demagogic lying".

Kenzo Tange's work in the second part of the 1950s, particularly his Kagawa Prefectural Office of 1956 (the project with which Japan definitively entered the international architectural forum) significantly contributed to the specific post-war development of regionalism and to the attempt to redefine modern architecture in an exchange that took place in 1959 when the building was presented at the Otterlo meeting of CIAM. Tange's response to Ernesto Rogers' enthusiastic praise of the building's regionalism as "a very good example of what we have to do", was guarded. "I cannot accept the concept of total regionalism," he asserted, adding that "tradition can be developed through challenging its own shortcomings," implying the same for regionalism.

This last statement of Tange's encapsulates the antinomy in the thinking - partly an attachment to, partly a rejection of - regional elements, that is typically behind the current practice of what we have called critical regionalism. This antinomy is the second essential element of the definition of critical regionalism. "Critical" here does not connote a "confrontational" attitude only. After all, as we have seen, Mumford's post-war regionalism was confrontational with respect to façadist, anomic, atopic modernism and the attitude of romantic 19th century regionalists was in open rebellion against the "imperialist" spread of the classical canon. But this does not necessarily make them critical in the more specialised sense we now apply, of a regionalism that is self-examining, self-questioning, self-evaluating; confrontational not only with regard to the world but also to itself.

The use of "critical" in this second sense originated in the serene essays of Kant[16] and is developed in the agitated writings of the Frankfurt School.[17] Critical works challenge not just the established actual world, as confrontational works do, but the very legitimacy of the possible world views that interpret it in the mind. One might say, borrowing Habermas's expression, that they "dissolve the objective illusion" in architecture. This occurs when a building is self-reflective, self-referential; when it contains, in addition to explicit statements, implicit **metastatements** that make the beholder aware of the artificiality of her or his way of looking at the world.

An essential characteristic of critical regionalist buildings, then, is that they are critical in two senses. In addition to providing contrasting images to the anomic, atopic, misanthropic features of a large number of current mainstream projects constructed worldwide, they raise questions in the viewer's mind about the legitimacy of the very regionalist tradition to which they belong.

The poetics of critical regionalism carries out its self-reflective function through the method of "defamiliarisation", a concept coined by the Russian literary theoretician Victor Shklovsky.[18] It was initially applied to literature but it can also be applied to architecture, as we have demonstrated in our studies on classical architecture.[19] But as it relates to regionalism, defamiliarization is useful only in regionalism's current critical phase.

Romantic regionalism, despite its confrontational stance, employed familiarisation. It selected regional elements linked in memory with forlorn eras and inserted them into new buildings, constructing scenographic settings for arousing "affinity" and "sympathy" in the viewer, forming familiarised scenes that, although contrasting, mostly emotionally, with despotic architecture, rendered consciousness insensible. The mawkish, gushing, sentimental regionalism with its overfamiliarising, immediate, easy, titillating, "as if", narcissistic *Heimat* settings, has had an even more narcotic - if not hallucinatory - effect on consciousness.

More polemically even than in the 1950s critical regionalism reacts against this explosion of counterfeit regionalist settings which are even more widespread in their commercial version today than they were in their totalitarian one in the 1930s. It selects regional elements for their potential to act as support, physical or conceptual, for human contact and community - what we may call "place-defining" elements - and incorporates them "strangely" rather than "familiarly". In other words, it makes them appear distant, hard to grasp, difficult, even disturbing. It frames, as it were, the sense of place in a strange sense of displacement. It disrupts the sentimental "embrace" between buildings and their consumers, "de-automatising" perception and thus "pricking the conscience", to use another of Shklovsky's expressions. Hence, through appropriately chosen poetic devices of familiarisation critical regionalism makes the building appear to enter into an imagined dialogue with the viewer. It sets up a process of hard cognitive negotiation in place of the fantasised surrender that follows from familiarisation and the seduction that follows from overfamiliarisation. It leads the viewer to a **metacognitive** state, a "democracy of experience", as Jerome Bruner might have called it; it conjures up a "forum of possible worlds".[20]

In contrast with previous phases of regionalism, current critical regionalism, emerging with Mumford's censoring of the fake modernism of the International Style, does not support the emancipation of one regional group nor does it set up one group against another. It tries to forge the identity of a "global group" in opposition to "them", "them" being the alien occupation army of technocracy and bureaucracy imposing the illegitimate rule of anomie and atopy. Furthermore, critical regionalism alerts us, through the poetics of its forms, not only to the loss of place and community but also to our "reflective" inability to become aware of this loss while it was occurring. Its relation to a global practice of architecture is also special. The operations of identifying, decomposing and recomposing regional elements in a "defamiliarising" way are part of the universal set of skills of architects. They can be carried out by any knowledgeable, responsible, competent architect committed to the understanding of local constraints. Critical regionalism does not imply professional parochialism.

In this brief sketch of the poetics of critical regionalism we have not tried to identify any general criteria of style. We have not provided answers to pragmatic questions such as "are wooden houses less atopic than concrete ones?" or "are concrete cafeterias more anomic than brick ones?" We have not made checklists of physical design criteria for how to be a critical regionalist. And for a good reason. The poetics of critical regionalism does not include a set of design rules of partitioning, motifs and genera as do classicism, the picturesque or De Stijl. Rather, as with *Neue Sachlichkeit* architecture, it draws its forms from the context. In other words its general poetics become specific, drawing from the regional circumscribed constraints that have produced places and collective representation in a given area. To cite just one example, in the case of Spanish critical regionalism these design elements include the prismatic purity and vivid colour of jointless brick façades; the inner courts of apartment houses called *corrala*; the *manzana* patios; the *miradores*. These are regional elements that are historically linked with the formation of a concrete urban *genius loci but* which are selected, defamiliarised and recomposed in new projects.[21]

There is also another mode in critical regionalist poetics, found more often in the United States, through which regional characteristics - natural rather than cultural - enter into design. This is the case of composing buildings optimally as shelters, respecting regional environmental constraints and accepting regional resources. This is the reverse of the anomie and atopy that result when nature is violated through brute force in order to control environmental conditions - not force as such, but as the result of the *hubris* of mind spent on nothing, a *hubris* present even when money and machinery are available, combined with the hubris of the mean view of the world that the project in its "gluttony" implies. In other words "placeness" and the containment of anomie and atopy are supported by the implicit messages of a well-tempered, "economical", "ecological" design.

Looking at one of these buildings, one cannot say that this is a well-formed critical regionalist building - as, for instance, one can say of a well-formed classical temple, this is a well-formed classical building. Kenneth Frampton, the critic whose writings have helped raise and spread the issue of critical regionalism more than any other today, has made this point very clearly:

> "The fundamental strategy of Critical Regionalism is to mediate the impact of universal civilisation with elements derived indirectly from the peculiarities of a particular place. It is clear from the above that Critical Regionalism depends upon maintaining a high level of critical self-consciousness. It may find its governing inspiration in such things as the range and quality of the local light, or in a tectonic derived from a peculiar structural mode, or in the topography of a given site."[22]

We have not tried to argue that critical regionalism should be seen as contradictory to trends towards higher technology and a more global economy and culture. It opposes merely their undesirable effects, the products of private interests and public mindlessness.

It seems that after two highly creative but also frustrating decades, during which architecture has oscillated between dreaming socially engaged visions completely outside the conceptual and practical framework of architecture and actualising socially vacuous exercises within the autonomous formal framework of architecture, we are coming closer to a more balanced outlook, closer to reality. One of the issues that identifies this new outlook is the problem of the architecture of place, the articulation of a critical statement, in terms of shape and space, about community in a world of global mobility and integration. Critical regionalism appears as a movement seriously engaged with this problem. This gives us enough ground to claim that it has emerged as one of the most exciting approaches in architecture today.

NOTES

1   See Alexander Tzonis and Liane Lefaivre, **The grid and the pathway** in **Architecture in Greece**, (1981, No 5) and A. Tzonis, L. Lefaivre and A. Alofsin, **Die Frage des Regionalismus**, N. Andritzky, L. Burckhardt and O. Hoffman, eds., **Für eine andere Architektur** (Fischer, Frankfurt 1981) Band 1, pp.121-134. See also K Frampton's important **Towards a critical regionalism**, in Hal Foster, ed., **The Anti-Aesthetic: Essays on Post-Modern Culture** (Bay Press, Seattle, U.S.A. 1983), pp. 16-30.

2   See Goethe's **Von deutscher Baukunst**, trs. N. Pevsner, in **Architectural Review. XCVIII**, pp.155ff. In the text Goethe argues, erroneously, that the Gothic was German. In fact the Gothic was French. It is generally accepted that the first Gothic building was the abbey church of St. Denis in the Ile de France, supervised by the abbot Suger for his patrons, the Capetian dynasty. For a general background on the subject of the role of Goethe in the Gothic revival in Germany see W. D. Robson-Scott, **The Literary Background of the Gothic Revival in Germany** (Oxford University Press, Oxford, 1965).

3   This point has been made by Jacques Gubler in his penetrating study **Viollet-le-Duc et l'Architecture Rurale**, in the exhibition catalogue **Viollet-le-Duc, Centenaire de la Mort a Lausanne** (Exposition au Musêe de l'Ancien Evéche, Lausanne, 1979).

4   For an outline of the biography of regionalism starting from its earliest "emblematic" phase in the early Renaissance and continuing through to the picturesque regionalism of the 18th century and the Romantic regionalism of the 19th century, see our

El Regionalismo critico y la arquitectura espanola actual, in **A &
V** (No. 3, Madrid 1985), pp. 4-19.

5   Proust translated Ruskin's **Bible of Amiens** into French, and the
overt and implicit references to Ruskin in **A la recherche du
temps perdu** constitute an important pattern in the fabric of the
novel. For an indication of the extent of Ruskin's influence on
Proust see the excellent **Marcel Proust, On reading Ruskin**,
edited and translated by J. Autret, W. Burford, P. Wolfe and
introduced by R. Macksey (Yale University Press, New Haven,
1987).

6   Patrick Geddes, **Cities in Evolution** (London, 1915).

7   Jean Gottmann, **Megalopolis** (MIT Press, Cambridge, Mass.,
U.S.A. 1961).

8   Melvin Webber, **The Urban Place and the Nonplace Urban
Realm** in M. Webber et al., eds., **Explorations into Urban
Structure** (University of Pennylvania Press, Philadelphia, 1964)
pp. 79-137. For a contemporary extensive critique of the Webber
thesis see S. Chermayeff and A. Tzonis, **Advanced Studies in
Urban Environments** (Yale University Press, New Haven, 1967).

9   Lewis Mumford, **The South in Architecture** (Harcourt, Brace &
Co., New York, 1941).

10   Lewis Mumford, **Skyline**, in the **New Yorker** (October 11th, 1947).

11   **The Museum of Modern Art Bulletin** (Spring 1948) pp. 35ff.

12   *Ibid*, p. 18.

13   *Ibid*, p. 9.

14   See **Architect's Year Book** (No. 8, 1957).

15   New Monumentality is an expression coined by Siegfried Giedion
for the monumental architecture of the early 1950s.

16   Immanuel Kant, **The Critique of Pure Reason** (1791).

17   For a synoptic coverage of the development of the idea of a critical
theory see Raymond Geuss, **The Idea of a Critical Theory:**

Habermas and the Frankfurt School (Cambridge University Press, Cambridge, 1981).

18   Shklovsky was a member of the "Russian Formalists", the avant-garde group of literary theoreticians active around the time of the Russian revolution. See Shklovsky's **Art as technique**, in L.T. Lemon and M. Reis, eds., **Russian Formalist Critique**,(University of Nebraska Press, Lincoln, 1965).

19   Alexander Tzonis and Liane Lefaivre, **Classical Architecture: The Poetics of Order**, (MIT Press, Cambridge Mass., USA, 1986). See in particular the last chapter, **Critical Classicism: the tragic function**.

20   Jerome Bruner, **Actual Minds, Possible Worlds** (Harvard University Press, Cambridge Mass., USA, 1986).

21   See our "**El regionalismo critico y la Arquitectura espanola actual**" in **A&V**, (No.3, Madrid, 1985) pp. 4-19.

22   K. Frampton, **Towards a Critical Regionalism: Six Points for an Architecture of Resistance**, in Hal Foster, ed., op. cit., p. 21.

V

THE INTERDISCIPLINARY FIELD OF FINE ART

Nicholas de Ville

Interdisciplinarity Discovered

In a spirit of contrariness, and as a response to the pedagogic trend towards interdisciplinarity (which I will try to describe in the first part of this paper), I want to act as an advocate for fine art as a subject in itself and, to a significant extent, for itself. Not art for art's sake, but rather art not forsaking art. In doing this it may appear that I am being as extreme as to argue against fine art as an interdisciplinary field. Not so. Rather, what I wish to focus on in this essay is the issue of boundary, which is also to reflect on the status of art, and the place of the art object, in the modern world. It is also to speak for art - its very particular imperatives, traditions and complex sense of itself - as something distinct, extreme and not collapsible into a generalised Art and Design field, nor into the spectacular entertainments of popular culture.

The first question such an approach provokes is: what is the discipline of which we speak in "interdisciplinary"?

Interdisciplinary is a couplet of terms that embody an internal tension: inter meaning between and disciplinary referring to the idea of the disciplines (also to discipline with its sense of restraint, and even punishment). Some writers, notably Foucault and Deleuze, have given disciplines the status of a central element in the regulation of social organisation in the 19th and early 20th centuries. For Deleuze their time is past; we have left the disciplinary societies to enter the societies of control.[1] For him the "enclosures" by which the disciplinary societies organise themselves - prison, hospital, school, family - are in crisis. So, too, are the disciplines themselves, whether they be scholarly or professional.

Today the liberal arts model of the university, at least, can be seen to be less and less dominated by the disciplines. However, it is important to question the nature of Deleuze's crisis. Is the subdivision of medicine into an ever-greater number of specialisms symptomatic of the same crisis as the drive towards interdisciplinarity in the liberal arts and the humanities? And where, if at all, does fine art fit into such a spectrum? The accusation of elitism that is levelled at the old disciplines has also been directed at fine art. Some art education administrators have dropped the term "fine art" from course descriptions on the grounds that it is redolent of elitist forms of cultural practice. Should all of us concerned with teaching fine art be thinking of doing the same? What is the price of the disintegration of the taxonomy? We can appreciate that we are entering difficult terrain when we ask: what is it about the shape of fine art pedagogy that we should be seeking to preserve? And what should we be eager to reform? Yet it is only when we ask ourselves these kinds of questions that we can begin to see before us the future requirements of fine art education.

Firstly, it is necessary to refresh our memory about some of the principles that have guided the shaping of undergraduate fine art programmes within the higher education sector. In order to understand the core principles enshrined in the national provision of fine art education we need to refer to the 1970 Report of a Joint Committee of the National Advisory Council on Art Education and the National Council for Diplomas in Art and Design, otherwise known as the Coldstream Report (this is the second of the two reports chaired by William Coldstream). In this report we can see the germination of many of the institutional habits and assumptions that underlie the structure of present-day fine art undergraduate programmes.

The most significant paragraphs, which outline the recommendations for the future of undergraduate fine art education, numbered 23, 24, 25 and 26, are worth quoting at length:

"23. We conclude that in its next phase of development the Diploma course system should allow for two distinct course structures. The first of these would be provided by the continued operation of courses similar in form to the present Dip AD courses but modified to permit a greater flexibility of approach. These are referred to as Group A courses..." (Fine art is a Group A course.)

"Group A courses.
24. In considering this proposed group of courses, we looked critically at the present concept of the four areas into which study for the Dip AD are divided, namely Fine Art, Graphic Design, Three Dimensional Design and Textiles/Fashion. On the whole, it seems to us to be useful to retain these four areas of study because they provide a convenient classification to which to relate the staffing administration and allocation of resources within a college as a whole. However, we affirm that from the viewpoint of education these four areas are not discrete and courses need not necessarily be confined to one of them.

"25....We envisage a more fluid system in which students may, if appropriate, pursue a broad range of studies which cross and overlap the boundaries of chief studies as hitherto conceived. This would not affect the main character of studies for the majority of students. It would extend the opportunity for students within a given area to enjoy a wider experience than has generally been possible hitherto."

With particular reference to fine art the report continues in paragraph 26:

"Whilst painting and sculpture or a combination of the two will, we expect, continue to be the main preoccupation of students in this area, we do not believe that studies in fine art can be adequately defined in terms of chief studies related to media. We believe that studies in fine art derive from an attitude which may be expressed in many ways. Their precise nature will depend upon the circumstances of individual colleges."[2]

It can be seen that the report offers a somewhat paradoxical view of fine art education. It is a view that seems to support the retention of "main" studies "for the majority of students" whilst at the same time encouraging "a more fluid system" and "a broad range of studies" (paragraph 25).

It is also notable that although the four subjects in group A courses are not "discrete", and courses "need not necessarily be confined to one of them", there is a clear indication elsewhere in the report that fine art is not now considered "central to all studies in the design field."[3]

The ethos of art education over the past twenty or so years has been based on the approach outlined in this report. The rather diffuse and imprecise nature of its advice, open to a variety of interpretations by art institutions, explains some of the diversity that can still be seen in fine art programmes. In some programmes no aspect of the making process - not least the pivotal relationship between form and content - has been constrained (at least in terms of pedagogic principles) by the subdivision of the subject into disciplines. In pursuit of this ideal many schools have diminished to the vestige of a division of labour the separate, discipline-led provinces of the "painting school" and the "sculpture school". Rather than labouring these categories - even when they do remain as vestigial institutional structures - art courses have (apart from a few determined exceptions) seen an individual student's fine art practice as being situated within a continuous interdisciplinary field where the form of the student's work may be sculpture or painting, but is just as likely to be photography, video or performance. Not only this, but working with any of these media is no guarantee that the next piece of work by the student will be expressed through the same medium.

I now want to turn from the consideration of the roots of today's fine art pedagogic practices to the way in which those practices are most tellingly expressed now. In today's programme descriptions we shall find the hesitant openness of Coldstream's report developed and its competing principles given new emphasis.

A good place to start is The Art and Design Directory.[4] This is a comprehensive catalogue of undergraduate programme descriptions published yearly. In the directory institutions offer brief outlines of the distinctive features of their programmes. Even cursory examination shows that "interdisciplinarity" is a term that appears in a significant number of course descriptions. In the 1993 edition out of 35 ADAR (Art and Design Admissions Registry) recruiting fine art programmes, eight explicitly mention interdisciplinarity; another fourteen descriptions imply interdisciplinarity (a few appear to offer an option of either specialised or interdisciplinary study) only eight are clearly discipline-led and another five have no programme description whatsoever.

Concerning interdisciplinarity we can read, for example: "every effort is made to foster an understanding of common fine art problems and to encourage interdisciplinary dialogue." Another institution offers "opportunities to explore interdisciplinary relationships between painting and sculpture". A third describes its BA (Hons) Fine Art programme as follows: "once the introductory phase is over students then have the option of working in or across any of the courses' [*sic*] disciplines which would seem appropriate for the expression of their ideas."

A fourth fine art programme states that "students are free to take from any disciplines whatever is necessary for the development of their studies: to work beyond or within 'traditional' boundaries". Similarly, a fifth description says that "initially students are introduced to all areas of the course through progressing an idea through positive interaction between areas. Each course unit encourages this interdisciplinary process which gives students a rich background in all areas while enabling them to specialize where this is appropriate." One BA (Hons) Fine Art programme offers "opportunities to explore interdisciplinary relationships between painting and sculpture", whilst another claims that the "course structure aims to develop abilities in the broad relationships and interdisciplines of fine art with facilities available to provide either 'broad-based' or 'specialist' study". Yet another states that "every effort is made to foster an understanding of common fine art problems and to encourage interdisciplinary dialogue".

In addition to the central place that the word "interdisciplinary" and its derivatives has in these and many similar course descriptions, we can also discover that other programmes offer unstructured curricula whereby the onus is on the student to design his or her own course from many options. While this is an expected feature of the newer modular degrees, it is also a fairly well-entrenched aspect of the older single honours programmes. Thus we can read of a BA Fine Art programme that "offers a wide choice of subjects for the historical, theoretical and critical studies elements of the course in the second and third years". This programme description also states that "for the greater part of their period at the institution fine art students have to shoulder the responsibility of planning their own work schedules and the nature and direction of their art practice is in great part determined by each individual student".

Several programme descriptions use confusing terms such as "interdisciplinary specialisation" or "multi-discipline specialization". Others suggest that they present the student with complex decisions to make about the learning possibilities, as in: "under the Fine Art umbrella students gravitate towards single, multi or interdisciplinary specialisation." We are invited to envisage the openness of "a broad-based Fine Art course where students are encouraged to take advantage of all media specialisms".

Only eight of the ADAR BA Fine Art programmes listed in the directory state that they maintain the traditional distinctions between disciplines. One such institution states: "students...are offered places on the Painting course because they indicate that they are committed to painting." A like-minded institution describes its BA (Hons) Fine Art programme thus: "this course is in effect two discrete courses: Painting and Sculpture...Those selected for this course (Painting) are expected to be potential painters..." Similarly on another BA (Hons) Fine Art programme "students specialise in depth within their chosen area..."

The significant majority of institutions whose fine art degree programmes emphasise the interdisciplinary approach to fine art education seem to assume that there is a fairly easily defined subject here: what we might term an interdisciplinary field of fine art practice.

The directory also describes a second group of undergraduate degree programmes that offer fine art as part of a larger field of study. In this category the academics responsible have concluded that fine art can be profitably studied at undergraduate level as part of an interdisciplinary field much larger (and more open) than the one evoked by BA Fine Art programmes. In university parlance these are interdisciplinary degrees, rather than single subject degrees. These interdisciplinary degrees have titles such as "Visual Performance", "Creative Arts", "Expressive and Performing Arts", "Fine Art, Sound and Image Option", "Visual and Performing Arts", "Interactive Arts", "BA (Hons) Art Design and Visual Communication", "BA (Hons) Art and Design (Joint Honours)" and "BA (Hons) Combined Studies (Art and Design)".

In the description of one university's BA (Hons) Visual Arts programme we read of "the need to integrate art into a wider public arena and to look for new relationships and partnerships based upon the principles of development, negotiation, collaboration and intervention..." Another university offers a BA Fine Art with Language. "This course promotes interaction between Fine Art disciplines and even in the final year many students are combining two or more disciplines in their practice. Students are encouraged to pursue ideas and themes in visual and verbal language and to develop a critical understanding of the similarities and differences between verbal and visual modes of representation." The same institution also offers a BA (Hons) Combined Arts in which Art and Design can be combined with "Media Studies, Theatre Arts, English, Education, History". It goes on to say that: "this course is designed for the kind of student who has a lively inquisitive mind and who doesn't like to be tied down within the confines of a single discipline from the start of studies." For a Modular Degree in Visual Studies, visual studies must be combined with "Dance, Drama, Education, English, English Language, Environmental Studies, French, Geography, History, Music, Psychology, Social Administration, Theology and Religious Studies, ID Studies". A BA (Hons) Art and

Related Arts programme states: "students specialise in Art, Dance, English or Music and this study will comprise 50% of the degree. The remaining half is Related Arts, studied by all Related Arts students together, thus bringing together Art, Dance, English and Music specialists. The aim is to explore the inter-relationships and interactions between the arts, mutual influences and to enable students to extend this specialism through collaborative work."[5]

The impression gained in reading these programme descriptions is that there is a kind of madness for interdisciplinarity in the air - and this is not confined to academia alone. To make the point, a quotation from the subscription advertisement for a new magazine called **Hybrid**:

> "Not all art forms are pure or thoroughbred. Some are hybrids...One striking and central significance hybrid art forms have, and which partly explains their appeal to and pursuit by artists, is this. Hybrid art forms, and the works they encompass, tend to be symbols of creativity itself, of forcefully and purposefully putting things together, of welding items previously disparate and unconnected into new and more complex unities."[6]

A further example will perhaps suffice to complete the impression. A conference synopsis from France:

> "A two-day reflection around the artistic and pedagogical project of Le Fresnoy. This conference will be above all the opportunity to open an exchange of ideas on experimental dimensions of teaching for artists based on dialogue between disciplines.
>
> By cross-fertilisation, we mean mutual impregnation, contributions and borrowings, shapes transfers, transversality, contamination, ie creation of a horizontal surface where interpenetration of cultures or references, of languages of techniques, makes up for excessive, unbearable pressure of verticality in which each medium coops itself up, as it is the case, for example, for today French cinema, too seldom turned toward formal and visual invention [*sic*]."[7]

It can be seen from the tenor of these quotations that "interdisciplinarity" as an idea and a term has become very significant for the creative arts in general, and fine art in particular. Not only has it become a widely used term to describe the aspirations of undergraduate fine art programmes, but also fine art is increasingly being seen, for educational purposes, as part of a larger interdisciplinary arts/humanities/social science field.

To sum up, it can be seen that "interdisciplinary" describes the complex field of contemporary fine art practice, a field that consists not just of painting and sculpture (which we might, perhaps, think of as the ancient disciplines of fine art practice), but also of photography, audio-visual media such as film and video, performance and installation - and then manifestations that combine elements from all these categories. This we can think of as fine art's internalised sense of interdisciplinarity.

Furthermore, there is also an important sense in which "interdisciplinary" is used to describe the zone between art and something else (or perhaps everything else) where art becomes non-art or, optimistically, new art; where the principles of art can be used to infuse other subjects with a new creative approach.

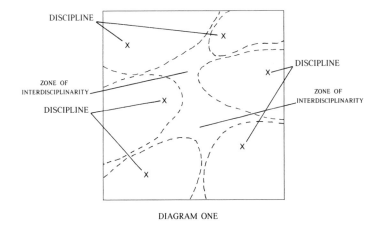

DIAGRAM ONE

A diagram that would capture the picture that the two senses of interdisciplinarity suggest might look something like this:

Such a diagram suggests that one possible danger might be that should the interdisciplinary field become sufficiently open it will begin to lose even the hesitant features we see above. It would be possible to dismantle, de-discipline, de-institutionalise the interdisciplinary field to the point where its diagrammatic representation would simply be a blank.

DIAGRAM TWO

Anyone who has been to an art school will recall the strange sensation of being confronted by a plain sheet of paper in a drawing lesson. The first question that arises is: why make a mark at all? What impels any particular course of action? Not only for what, but against what - next to what - do I start? Here, I would suggest, we are confronted by the epistemological nightmare. Diagrams may not be essential prerequisites for understanding, but the epistemological nightmare is to find information everywhere but not to have the means by which to turn it into anything useful, structured, ethical. In art, realism is the consequence of the flight from that dilemma; this explains the habitual response to the drawing-class impasse: draw a dried teasel.

Interdisciplinarity Defined (As Ideology)

In the previous section I attempted to demonstrate the central place "interdisciplinary" has come to have in the brief descriptions used to characterise the fine art programmes listed in **The Art and Design Directory**. I would like now to pursue the significance of the term in some detail. In particular I want to show how it is part of a larger philosophical and sociological project. This project has come to be one of the most significant strands of critical resistance to the kind of society we find in the West and it is important to consider interdisciplinarity as a strategy that is, to a significant degree, a response to a broad critique of the institutions of knowledge, and of institutional oppression.

Colin Cina's report on the working group that he chaired at the European League of Institutes of the Arts conference (Strasbourg, November 1992) is a good starting ponit for this investigation. The working group was called Experiences and Problematics of Inter-Disciplinarity. This is part of his report:

> "At Higher Education levels, we seemed to have reached a situation where Inter-Disciplinarity, in its various Post-Modernist constructions, can either exist as an operative device which shapes educational structures - e.g., offering students a range of study choices in cognate areas ("the Expressive Arts Syllabus") - but essentially through the potential it holds to manifest itself as an ideal; a pre-visioning of a potential for new artists literally to form new "language" from a de-disciplined process of Arts study and to progress to innovate forms of professional outcomes."[8]

Going through **The Art and Design Directory** one has a suspicion that many of those using the word "interdisciplinary" are doing so in the first sense of "a range of study choices in cognate areas". It is worth noting that this first definition is very much a restatement of the sense of interdisciplinarity that is central to the Coldstream Report of 1970:

> "We consider it desirable wherever practicable to eliminate within the areas any rigid concept of separate chief studies. Instead we envisage a more fluid system in which students

> may, if appropriate, pursue a broader range of studies
> which cross or overlap the boundaries of chief studies as
> hitherto conceived."[9]

However, for those fine art programmes pursuing a strong
ideological expression of interdisciplinarity it is the second of Cina's two
definitions that is to the fore. It is also worth considering whether it is
possible to keep these two versions of interdisciplinarity apart. Perhaps
it cannot be a matter of either/or: the implications of the second
definition inevitably infect the first, and it is the implications of Colin
Cina's second, more radical meaning that we must follow because it
draws on theories that are not only critical of the scope and discrete
nature of existing disciplines, but also of the nature of the present-day
educational institution.

The following excerpt from the programme description for the BA in
Visual Performance offered by Dartington College takes up the theme of
questioning the existing disciplines:

> "It [the programme] examines theoretical models provided
> by the historical development of modernism, performance
> theory arising from pre-industrial ritual, and methods of
> focusing on the connecting strands between specialisms
> provided by current cultural theories such as
> post-structuralism. Visual Performance at Dartington
> occupies an 'awkward' position in relation to established
> disciplines and reflects a serious engagement with
> pluralism."[10]

We can note as significant in this description the theoretical
underpinning of interdisciplinarity by current cultural theories such as
post-structuralism. We should also highlight the implication that
disciplines are characteristic of a monoculture. Also the educational
necessity of taking up an "awkward" relationship to disciplines, and
perhaps the implication that such a stance enables a distancing from
modernism.

All these topics have considerable resonance to anybody working in
art education: they are significant issues in any critical theory
programme. For the theoretical agendas that raise these questions it is,

at root, institutions' power over knowledge that is at issue. What is being articulated is the idea that educational institutions need to divest themselves of some of the senses of authority that have arisen as a consequence of modernist thinking. In passing from the period of modernism to one that is post-modernist in spirit we are now able to see some of the assumptions of modernism that formerly were hidden. The process of transition, which the academic world has been engaged with for some time now, is described by Steven Connor in these terms:

> "First of all, each discipline produced more and more
> conclusive evidence of the existence of postmodernism
> within its own area of cultural practice; secondly, and really
> more importantly, each discipline drew progressively upon
> the discoveries and definitions made in other disciplines.
> With the appearance of Jean-François Lyotard's **La
> Condition Postmoderne** in 1979, and its translation into
> English in 1984, these different disciplinary diagnoses
> received an interdisciplinary confirmation, and there no
> longer seemed room for disagreement that postmodernism
> and postmodernity had come to stay."[11]

We have here, then, a purposeful link being made between interdisciplinarity as a method of research and a new era of intellectual thought termed post-modern. This is Lyotard's description of the virtues of interdisciplinarity from **The Postmodern Condition**:

> "If education must not only provide for the reproduction of
> skills, but also for their progress, then it follows that the
> transmission of knowledge should not be limited to the
> transmission of information, but should include training of
> all the procedures that can increase one's ability to connect
> fields jealously guarded from one another by the traditional
> organization of knowledge. The slogan of "interdisciplinary
> studies", which became particularly popular after the crisis
> of 1968 (two years before the second Coldstream Report)
> but was being advocated long before that, seems to move in
> this direction..."[12]

And then, a little later:

> "The idea of an interdisciplinary approach is specific to the age of delegitimation and its hurried empiricism. The relation to knowledge is not articulated in terms of the realization of the life of the spirit or the emancipation of humanity, but in terms of the users of a complex conceptual and material machinery and those who benefit from its performance capabilities. They have at their disposal no metalanguage or metanarrative in which to formulate the final goal and correct use of that machinery. But they do have brainstorming to improve its performance."[13]

Lyotard has seen the examination of the contemporary organisation of knowledge and its institutions to be one of the most important tasks for analytical thinking. For him, as for others such as Derrida, Foucault and Deleuze, the idea of interdisciplinarity is not only associated with learning in a post-modern world but is also a strategic response to existing academic institutions and their organisation of knowledge.

Edward Said has also concerned himself with a critique of contemporary academia. For him it is the pervasive political and social implications of the traditional disciplines that open up a critical view of the organisation of the university:

> "It is patently true that, even within the atomized order of disciplines and fields, methodological investigations can and indeed do occur. But the prevailing mode of intellectual discourse is militantly antimethodological, if by methodological we mean a questioning of the structure of fields and discourses themselves. A principle of silent exclusion operates within and at the boundaries of discourse; this has now become so internalized that fields, disciplines and their discourses have taken on the status of immutable durability. Licensed members of the field, which has all the trappings of a social institution, are identifiable as belonging to a guild, and for them words like 'expert' and 'objective' have an important resonance. To acquire a position of authority within the field is, however, to be involved internally in the formation of a canon, which usually turns out to be a blocking device for methodological and disciplinary self questioning."[14]

Fine Art and Interdisciplinarity

What is under review in this body of critical thinking, then, are canons, categories, disciplines and their areas of competence. Yet there is another leap to be made here, and that is to put art under the same critical scrutiny as though it, too, were in some unproblematic sense a discipline. The mechanisms of this scrutiny are made very clear by Hal Foster in his essay **(Post)Modern Polemics**":

> "What self-criticism is to modernist practice, deconstruction is to postmodernist practice. If the 'essence' of modernism is to use the methods of a discipline in order "to entrench it more firmly in its area of competence" (Greenberg), the 'essence' of postmodernism is to do the same but in order, precisely, to subvert the discipline. Postmodernist art 'disentrenches' its given medium, not only as an autonomous activity but also as a mode of representation with assured referential value and/or ontological status. In general, postmodernist art is concerned not with the formal purity of traditional artistic mediums, but with textual 'impurity' - the interconnections of power and knowledge in social representations. It is in these terms that the art object - indeed, the art field - has changed, as the old Enlightenment decorum of distinct forms of expression grounded in separate areas of competence, is no longer obeyed. And with this destructuring of the object and its field has come a decentering of the subject, both artist and audience."[15]

We can see how the analyses of writers like Lyotard and Said reach beyond the world of the university, and begin to inform critiques of all manner of fields. This is of particular significance for the art academy since it is exactly the balancing point between art and the institutions of knowledge that the art academy must occupy. It is under double scrutiny and double suspicion.

The force of this kind of critique is to give significantly negative attributes to the traditional categories of fine art - and by this I mean painting and sculpture. Foster employs Greenberg's exceedingly narrow characterisation of modernist painting as a cipher for modernism itself. In so doing he conflates Greenberg's academicism with the vested interests that Said vilifies in his attacks on academia. Is fine art really the same kind of academic field as those that figure so large in Said's mind? In seeing painting in a reductive, formalist light, Foster sets the scene for others to reduce painting to a formal symbol of the male-dominated tradition of art - and to split art's interdisciplinary field into diametrically opposed camps. In so doing, the danger is that it is the complex operations of the interdisciplinary field that are wrecked.

Foster is not alone in his analysis. Douglas Crimp makes a somewhat similar point, focusing, here, on artists whose specific aim he sees as being to rhetorise the critique of the institution:

> "Employing various strategies, these artists (Buren, Broodthaers, Serra, Haacke, Sherman, Levine and Lawler) have worked to reveal the social and material conditions of art's production and reception - those conditions that it has been the museum's function to dissemble. One could add to these artists a list of others who have turned to modes of production that are altogether incompatible with the museum's space, that seek new audiences, that attempt to construct a social praxis outside the museum's precincts. In short, 'my' postmodernism subjected the reigning idealism of mainstream modernism to a materialistic critique and thereby showed the museum - founded on the presuppositions of idealism - to be an outmoded institution, no longer having an easy relationship to innovative contemporary art."[16]

Other writers have extended this critique in their own terms. Thus, Jean Fisher:

> "...Eurocentric 'high art', its universalising principles, and the market and critical framework which support it, must be seen as a 'commodified language' that stands in antagonistic relation to vernaculars or 'other' symbolic systems. What interests me here, however, is whether the latter (the unpredictable, the heterogeneous, the dissenting - those 'inefficient' elements that disrupt the desired efficiency of society as a machine with a coherent national identity) are capable of sustaining any form of resistance

against commodification; whether, in fact, an 'emancipatory' practice is possible."[17]

Fisher describes the nature of this "emancipatory practice" as follows:

"By contrast, montage, heterogeneous media or the use of cross-cultural aesthetic codes, introduces a spatio-temporal component that opens art to models of transformability and narration; to an awareness on the part of the viewer of her involvement in the production of meaning; and to a re-evaluation of the body in art, not as 'nature' but as an inscription within the sociopolitical text. The effect of such practices has been to confront the tyranny of nouns standing for definable objects - 'Art' with a capital 'A' - with present participles of a performative function - making, acting, speaking, writing, storytelling, listening, seeing, feeling, imagining, and so on.

"Moreover, mediated technological practices, using reproductive techniques, (recycling, remixing, transmission, playback, virtual realities, etc.) are self-consciously inauthentic; they make no pretence of reflecting the order of the visible world as if it revealed some essential 'truth' of 'nature' - the mimetic assumption upon which Western art has classically been predicated."[18]

The remarks in these two excerpts, taken together, invite a reading in which painting and sculpture represent the Eurocentric high art that "must" be seen as "commodified" and "antagonistic" to vernaculars and other symbolic systems. When we add this thought to what has gone before we can see that the interdisciplinarity inherent in forms of media practice outlined above cannot be seen as having an easy relationship with the disciplines of painting or sculpture. Indeed, they are at war! The reason is clear: disciplines are the instruments of what Said characterises as repressive academic professionalism.

To recap, post-modern critique of academic institutions and professional disciplines demands new knowledge-gaining processes that are interdisciplinary in nature and antagonistic to the traditional notions of professional categories and disciplines. They are antagonistic because the traditional institutions are not liberating but oppressive.

They particularly oppress those not empowered within our kind of society: women, and ethnic and religious minorities. Interdisciplinarity as a critical stance leads to a theoretical position in which capitalism and fascism - intertwined - lie behind the oppressive nature of the institution. That means, as far as the fine art academy is concerned, that there is a battle going on between the normative disciplines - painting, sculpture, photography - and various interdisciplinary modes of making. Interdisciplinary studies in fine art are antagonistic to those categories and cannot be held in some easy relationship to them. These are the more extreme associations that interdisciplinarity carries with it.

In his essay **The End Of Painting** Crimp identifies the historical moment of the end of painting by citing Foucault's perception when looking at **Las Meninas**: "What Foucault sees when he looks at this painting, then, is the way representation functioned in the classical period, a period that came to an end, in Foucault's archaeological analysis of history, at the beginning of the nineteenth century, when our own age, the age of modernism, began. And of course, if this era of history came to an end, so too did its means of understanding."[19] (It seems that Crimp's fierce claim that painting is dead may be, in fact, merely saying that certain of its codes are moribund.)

The effect of these arguments on the interdisciplinary field of fine art has been twofold. Firstly they have rendered the disciplines difficult to support as components of the field. Secondly, (and this is far more pernicious) they have suggested that the field is, in fact, boundless and can be opened up for academic purposes as part of a vista termed "visual art" where modules of project-led activity bleed art into drama, typography into painting, dance into performance, into installation, into interior design, in a barely redeemed promiscuity of forms, styles and crossed wires. Although the imagination of the student, in some vertiginous sense, may be stimulated by an arena that is "a virtual envelopment by recyclones, voodoo economics, neo-nightmares, deathtrips, skin-swaps, teraflops, Winter-mute-wasted Turing-cops, sensitive silcon, socket-head subversion, polymorphic hybridizations, descending data-storms, and cyborg catwomen stalking amongst the screens"[20], it tends to make for brains of mangled floppy discs. We are in particular need of interpreters when academics start parodying techno-babble! Does it follow that it is necessarily academia's role to emulate the multi-media world of free-floating signification in its pedagogic practices? Even William Gibson considers it necessary to assimilate data into the kinds of pre-formed images that the disciplines suggest. "Put the trodes on and they were out there, all the data in the world stacked up like one big neon city, so you could cruise around and have a kind of grip on it, visually anyway, because if you didn't, it was too complicated, trying to find your way to a particular piece of data you needed."[21]

There is yet one more edifice of interpretation that has been built on the theoretical base outlined in the previous two sections. This has had the effect, not of making everything seem available but of making itself appear a collusion with reactionary forces. This development has occurred around very specific interpretations of themes developed by Deleuze and Guattari, particularly, in the book **Anti-Oedipus**. This work is very much a development of Foucault's interest in power and knowledge and, indeed, he wrote the preface to the book. Deleuze and Guattari build on Foucault's critique of institutions as oppressive entities. Furthermore, in **Anti-Oedipus** the repressive nature of institutions is closely linked to the desire to be repressed. In his introduction to **Anti-Oedipus** Foucault characterised it as a handbook that might show how to effect political interventions within the institution. Thus Foucault writes that **Anti-Oedipus** is an "introduction to the Non-Fascist Life...the fascism in us all, in our heads and in our everyday behaviour, the fascism that causes us to love power, to desire the very thing that dominates and exploits us."[22]

The partnership of Deleuze and Guattari owes something quite particular to Guattari's psychoanalytic background and his interest in the links between psychological repression and social oppression. In **Anti-Oedipus** we find capitalist production characterised as a pathological response to the notion - associated with Freud - that desire denotes a sense of lack. In attacking the meaning of desire in Freud's work they undertake a reappraisal of one of the founding assumptions of 20th-century psychoanalysis. They turn Freud's characterisation on its head and no longer see desire as lack. For them desire is production, it is produced by a component of the human subject they term "desiring-machines":

> "Desiring-machines are both technical and social. It is in this sense that desiring-production is the locus of aprimal psychic repression whereas social production is where social repression takes place, and it is between the former and the latter that there occurs something that resembles secondary psychic repression in the 'strictest' sense..."[23]

> "Desiring-machines...continually break down as they run, and in fact run only when they are not functioning properly: the product is always an offshoot of production, implanting itself upon it like a graft, and at the same time the parts of the machine are the fuel that makes it run."[24]

They view art as a special form of production that runs contrary to the principles of other forms of production under capitalist (anti)socialisation:

> "Art often takes advantage of this property of desire-machines by creating veritable group fantasies in which desiring-production is used to short-circuit social production, and to interfere with the reproductive function of technical machines by introducing an element of dysfunction."[25]

The following quotation reflects the importance of their work to critical theory:

> "It was Deleuze and Guattari's **Anti-Oedipus** which subverted the philosophical landscape by once again introducing the individual faced with history: to produce a work of art is to put desire in motion, which overcomes all models, pre-established orders and determinism, in order to give concrete form to potentiality and difference."[26]

There is a clear implication here, for painting and, to a lesser extent, for all art production that is object or convention based (disciplines as "models, pre-established orders"). The implication is that such forms of art production, because they are commodifiable, are implicated in capitalist lack and exploitation.

Deleuze and Guatarri's image of society under capitalism - as with many of the writers that I have quoted in this paper - is of a society lost in pathological symptoms. There is little respite from this except in terms of local strategies. As Foucault writes in his preface: "develop action, thought, and desires by proliferation, juxtaposition and disjunction, and not by subdivision and pyramidal hierarchization."[27]

It is problematic, to say the very least, that, in the light of Deleuze and Guattari's analysis, there is the potential here to interpret Foucault's strategy as best implemented by a withdrawal from all making - from all creative actions that might produce art objects - on the grounds that capitalism subjects absolutely any material thing to absolute commodification. Instead they are driven to attempt to present dematerialised art, the presence of which is guaranteed by virtue of the purposeful dysfunctioning of desiring-machines.[28]

Interdisciplinarity as Control

The trajectory of the arguments that I have tried to describe in the previous sections of this paper can be summarised by the accompanying diagram. What is most evident in the diagram is that as one goes down the page so the antagonism between disciplines - on the left - and interdisciplinarity - on the right - grows. It is curious that this antagonism comes about through a re-establishment of the simple binary terms that post-structuralist thought is always at such pains to disavow. We see a trajectory of theory produced by a galaxy of thinkers whose intention has been to offer a liberated - and liberating - view of contemporary culture, but this intention has been partially subverted. Where is that pluralism when binary antagonisms - explicitly repudiated in the aim of constructing an alternative to the model of Enlightenment thinking - are reintroduced, yet disavowed, in a cleansed model of discourse?

INTERDISCIPLINARITY AS PART OF A POST-STRUCTURALIST CRITIQUE OF THE FINE ART FIELD.

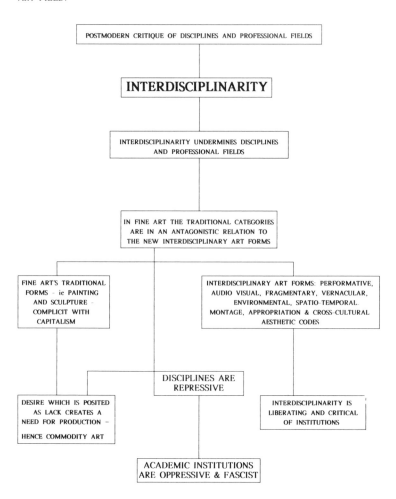

Derrida can be said to speak for many aspects of the post-structuralist project, so it is of particular relevance to take note when we find him discussing his own institution, The International College Of Philosophy, with Geoffrey Bennington at the ICA in 1985. He speaks of how people will become members of his college, and of their need to propose projects:

> "The projects should conform to the regulating idea of new objects, new themes and themes and objects which are not studied enough in universities and other current institutions. We do not mean by this that things that are taught and studied in the universities are not interesting, but as soon as they are recognised and identified as legitimate objects in other institutions, we are not specially interested in them. We are not at war with other institutions, but we select themes and objects that are marginalised or excluded or disqualified in other institutions..."[29]

> "Of course we do not believe in the opposition between liberal and non-liberal, we know it is very complicated and more and more complicated, and this complication is one of our concerns - not only in our minds but in the seminars which we organise..."[30]

> "We know that we cannot simply decide at the beginning that we won't be simply a liberal or a private or a public institution; but we keep in mind that this is a problem and that we want to change this situation and have a new approach to these problems."[31]

These short extracts are exemplary in that they seek both to define the interdisciplinary project and, also, to identify the internal doubts that interdisciplinarity must preserve about the extent of its own competences and the competences of forms of knowledge-seeking exercised elsewhere, and not least within the disciplines.

What is represented in the diagram is a crisis of interpretation for the fine art academy, and particularly for those responsible within the academy for the promulgation of theories that seek to set the creative individual in the context of the social. There is danger of a poisoned division between discipline and interdisciplinarity; a growing crisis of interpretation, because of which we are in danger of dissolving the fine art field and destroying any sense of there being disciplines within the field.

If this is to be the case, we can blame no one other than ourselves if fine art becomes a kind of adjunct to any other subject you care to think of. This is a crisis that is internal to our field, not one generated by external forces. The disciplines offer the sense of limitation and closure that interdisciplinary art forms refuse - but, none the less, they seem fated to remain within a redefined definition of the fine art field in order for their larger sense of cultural project to be identified.

We must accept that the interdisciplinary field will always bleed at the edges - not only that, but that the field must be thought of in relation to art's conceptual framing, and not in relation to its subject matter (which has a boundary no less than cognition itself).

What it is necessary to question, at this moment, is some general kind of thing termed "Visual Arts", offered for study at university level as a unitary field. It is important to speak against fine art and design as components of modular degree courses; and for fine art as an interdisciplinary field, but as an interdisciplinary field where it is interdisciplinarity and its definitions that are the very nub of the issue to be addressed. It is the inter that we must interrogate as well as disciplines.

This essay is not concerned with pedagogic policies, nor the practical strategies that might follow from a careful consideration of the interdisciplinary impulse, nor what role disciplines play in that impulse. Those are subjects for another paper. However, by way of a final thought, let me return to a phenomenon that I noted in my research into undergraduate fine art programmes: that some fine art courses have retained schools of painting and sculpture - or some other form of institutional indication of the persistence of the idea of disciplines - alongside the rhetoric of interdisciplinarity.

This, which appears, at first glance, to be the result of a badly thought through academic plan, might be, in fact, an institutional reflex designed to maintain some sense of a framework for the questioning that students must evolve if they are to be able to position their practice in the complex, seemingly structureless, visual environment in which they find themselves living - and in relation to which they wish to perform practical acts that are, in some way, critical.

Lastly, since this essay has been concerned, primarily, with how we interpret those texts that are significant for art-making, it seems worth reaffirming the principle that the art academy should strive to construct scenarios wherein students can see themselves not as a term in a one-dimensional world of opposing terms but rather as complex nucleic entities.

NOTES

1   G. Deleuze, **Postscript on the Societies of Control** (October No. 59, Winter 1991, MIT Press, Cambridge Mass.,USA), p. 3-7.

2   **The Structure of Art and Design Education in the Further Education Sector** Report of a Joint Committee of the National Advisory Council on Art Education and the National Council for Diplomas in Art and Design: (London, 1970).

3   *Ibid.*, para. 42.

4   M. Stallard, ed., **The Art and Design Directory for 1993 entry.** (Avec Designs Ltd., Bristol 1992).

5   The iteration of these fragments of programme descriptions is offered to give a broad impression of pedagogic principles. I have not sought to identify individual institutions, not so much to save the blushes of colleagues as to make the text flow more easily. Anyone with half an hour to spare may find these and many similar descriptions in **The Art and Design Directory** or any pile of prospectuses.

6   Jerrold Levinson, **Hybrid Art Forms** in **Journal of Aesthetic Education**. Quoted on publicity material for **Hybrid: The International Cross-Artform Bi-Monthly.**

7   From information pack for the conference **Pedagogy and Cross-Fertilisation of Disciplines** organised by Le Fresnoy, Studio National for Contemporary Art, Roubaix, France, November 1993.

8   Colin Cina, **Experiences and Problematics of Inter-Disciplinarity**, (European League of Institutes of the Arts, Strasbourg, November 1992) p. 44.

9   See Note 2.

10 From Dartington College's course information pack, March 1993.

11 Steven Connor, **Postmodernism and the Academy**, in **Post-modernist Culture** (Blackwell, Oxford, England and Cambridge Mass., U.S.A., 1989), p. 6.

12 Jean-François Lyotard, **The Postmodern Condition: The Theory and History of Literature** (Volume 10, Manchester University Press, 1984), p. 52.

13 *Ibid*, p. 52.

14 Edward Said, **Opponents, Audiences, Constituencies and Community** in Hal Foster, ed., **Postmodern Culture** (Pluto Press, London, 1983), p. 149.

15 Hal Foster, **(Post)Modern Polemics** in **Recodings: Art, Spectacle, Cultural Politics** (Bay Press, Seattle, U.S.A., 1985). p. 130.

16 Douglas Crimp, **The Postmodern Museum**, in **On The Museum's Ruins** (M.I.T. Press, Cambridge, Mass., U.S.A., London, England, 1993). p. 287.

17 Jean Fisher, **On Dis - Place - Ment** in **Place, Position, Presentation, Public** (Jan Van Eyck Akadamie, Holland, 1992). p. 271.

18 *Ibid*, p. 272.

19   Douglas Crimp, **The End of Painting** in **On the Museum's Ruins**.
      op. cit. p. 96.

20   Nick Land, **Machinic Desire,** in **Textual Practice**, (Volume 7,
      Cambridge University Press, 1993), p. 482.

21   Willian Gibson, **Mona Lisa Overdrive** (Grafton, London, 1989).
      p.22.

22   Michel Foucault, Preface to **Anti-Oedipus** (The Athlone Press,
      London 1984). p. xii.

23   G. Deleuze and F. Guattari, **Anti-Oedipus** (The Athlone Press,
      London, 1984). p. 32.

24   *Ibid.*, p. 31.

25   *Ibid.*, p. 32.

26   Nicolas Bourriaud, **Anti-Thinkers In The '80s**, in **Flash Art** (No.
      142, October 1988), p. 84.

27   Michel Foucault, *op. cit.*, p. xiii.

28   The following is offered by way of illustration. "If Andrea Fraser's
      output stops short of the production of finished objects, it is
      because her approach represents the development of a critical
      economy that serves to lay bear the political economy." in Frank
      Perrin, **Flash Art** (No. 175, March/April 1994). p. 45.

29   Jacques Derrida, (with Geoffrey Bennington) **On Colleges and
      Philosophy** in Lisa Appognanesi, ed., **Postmodernism** (ICA
      Documents, Free Association Books, London, 1989). p. 212.

30   *Ibid,.* p. 213.

31   *Ibid.*, p. 213.

VI

AN ARTIST LOOKS AT ART EDUCATION

Susan Hiller

When I was invited to participate in this conference[1] I agreed to speak on the understanding that I would "speak as an artist", because if artists don't speak about art education they leave the debate to theoreticians and educationalists, and this strikes me as extremely problematic. Already a great many people involved in art education in schools and colleges in this country, as administrators and as teachers, have no actual experience in art practice. From my point of view this seems as peculiar as it would be to teach French without being able to speak a word of it. Yet it is part of a pattern in many aspects of our society. Looking at art, reading about art, analysing art, theorising art and related activities are not the same as "doing" art, obviously. Yet this slide from *practice* to *theory*, from particular *experiences* to generalised *abstractions*, from the *dream* to the *word*, from *art* to *education* is often accepted almost unthinkingly by art educationists. I wondered what, speaking as an artist, I ought to, or indeed could, say about this. And I wondered, too, how best to speak so that my talking would not be heard simply as raw material for other discourses, as the speech of the native is appropriated by the anthropologist, or the dream of the patient is "written up" by the therapist. What I wanted was to establish a situation where an artist could speak as an expert among experts - but an expert on what, exactly?

This is what I decided would be different about an artist talking "about" art education. First, it would be very much "talking about", talking around the subject, trying to bring it into focus. Locating the subject, perhaps by emphasising the negative spaces around it, which shape it. Finding the subject but not cutting it off at the edges as though it were already neatly cropped and framed, as when one says, in words, "the body", or "the view from a window", or "three apples on a table", which are ways of not looking to find the subject but imagining it is already there, that you already know what it is. An artist talking would not necessarily be comfortably instructive but could be evocative. It could be a performative act, highlighting the essential contribution of the audience to the creation of meaning. And perhaps a way of distinguishing this way of talking from others would be to allow the different kinds of ways an artist things - the personal, perceptual, formal, social and theoretical - to emerge and problematise one another.

For instance, by beginning like this: I myself never had a proper art school education. Neither did the late Francis Bacon. This may well sum up the totality of what, as artists, we had in common... Of course, a great many other artists also did not go to art school or to academies or ateliers where art instruction was given. From the late 19th century onwards, although most artists did experience formal art training, some outstanding examples, if they went on to further education at all, might have attended a university where they did not study art or they might have arrived at art after trying other kinds of work, like Vincent van Gogh who had been a preacher and dealer in paintings, or Gauguin who was a merchant banker, etc. Of the people who did study art, a great many never became artists and didn't take up work in art-related fields, and the same is true today. So the conclusion here would have to be that art education is not essential to the training of artists, and that art education trains many students not to be artists.

Speaking personally, and still seeking to see the subject clearly, leads me to a bit of autobiography. When I first came to England to live in London more than twenty-five years ago, I had finished postgraduate work in anthropology and undertaken very unsystematic studies in art, ranging from postgraduate film courses to studio classes in drawing and painting at a variety of schools and colleges, some the equivalent of amateur evening classes and some intended for professional artists wanting to work in a group. I'd also done some very basic work with a famous master printer in France. I had worked in places at terrible jobs where I met other people who were writers, musicians, painters, performers, film makers, political organisers. I had begun to think very hard about the functions and meaning of art, and had produced paintings and some works with groups of people; my ideas were on the cusp between minimalism and Fluxus, heading for conceptualism. I had completely rejected the kind of painting that had been taught in the distinguished undergraduate women's college where I'd taken my degree - the kind of painting then called "the new humanism", a form of figurative work that was not at all new. (I felt it was backward looking, the kind of art I'd grown up with.)

But it was in London, for the first time since primary school, that I heard a painting called a "picture". It was an artist who said it. I was rather shocked. No one I knew in other countries would have used such a word. Mimesis and picturing were not issues elsewhere. So I did not take up a place at the Royal College of Art because I took this word seriously and believed I would have to fight those battles about figuration versus abstraction all over again on my own, and I didn't want to. These were no longer the relevant debates, as far as I was concerned, and I was afraid - I use this word quite deliberately, for it was real fear - of being distracted by them, held back, confused or discouraged...

Soon afterwards someone told me that "Paris has its artists' cafés, New York has artists' bars, and here in England...well, we have art colleges." It was at about that point that I began to see there was something else important about the British art college, namely its function as a professionalising or socialising body, a validating body. In the most profound sense. In the United States, most artists I knew had studied art in the context of an art department within a university, where criteria of professionalism did not automatically apply. But British art education, until recently, has been a rite of passage more than a form of training, a situation in which older artists influence, criticise and sponsor younger ones while the younger ones keep their elders on their toes.

Yet, curiously, I have always been glad I did not attend a British art college. I am certain that I would not have been one of the artists who would have been taken up and sponsored, and most likely I would have learnt not to be an artist. My gender is wrong, I am a foreigner, and in at least two other ways - which I will come to in a second - I have a different perspective. So I am grateful that I experienced a self-selected programme of educational bits ranging eclectically over a number of fields. This has, perhaps, compensated for the very great disadvantage that, in this country, without an institutional history and context, I have had to learn to survive without mentors. Perhaps because of this, as a teacher I have been very aware of my responsibility to sponsor and act as advocate for the new perspectives that I have witnessed emerging from incoherence into coherence in my own students, without trying to force them to locate themselves on an out-of-date map.

For, traditionally, in the British art college the mentorship of older artists has created divisive groups of students, each of which adopts attitudes or artistic commitments that *rename, without actually remapping,* the terrain defined by previous generations. The upheavals caused by acrimonious debates conducted in the name of abstraction or figuration, painting or conceptualism, cultural studies or art history, design or fine art, have engaged the energies of successive generations of tutors and students. A new two-sided debate inevitably rises, phoenix-like, from the ashes of previous arguments. And the old divisions and allegiances are retained under new names.

The way I see it, these arguments and debates don't occur in isolation in art colleges, but ought to be seen as part and parcel of the wider debates about power and representation within society. And that is one of the main ways in which my focus on the topic "art education" is a little different from that of most artist-teachers, because I see the art college as one site among many where specific struggles for visibility and recognition take place, and I see art practices and definitions as ways by which alternative futures are either enabled or disabled.

Now looking again from a different point of view, still through my own eyes, at these struggles for power within society as made visible within the art college as regards say, struggles over aspects of the curriculum or teaching methods, or as regards the antagonism between theoretical studies and craft-based or technical studio practices, or as regards notions of *training* versus notions of *educating* - behind all these contradictions, I see something else coming into focus. This is something rather interesting but hard to see, something that needs to be attended to but usually is not, something that has been overlooked in all the previous discussions today. My sense of this "something else" is another difference between my perception of the subject of art education and that of many other teachers in art colleges. This difference follows on from the first, that is, from my view that colleges of art are sites of contestation, but I would not define this contestation in political terms, *at least as this is commonly understood*. I think I see that something much, much more fundamental is at stake, something that is only represented by or is possibly even *masked* by predefining the issues as political in the usual sense...I can explain this by saying that I see politics, like the art college, as one site among many where basic cultural contradictions are expressed.

By refusing to recognise - as some professionals do - the reality of cultural dualisms, does not help to supersede or eliminate them. As has been said many times, it is quite possible that many perceived cultural contradictions are artefacts of binary aspects of the human body. The bodily artefact most relevant to art education, its place in our society, how it is seen, and what it does, is the development in the human brain of two asymmetrical hemispheres with different functions. In the brains of animals the cerebral hemispheres are symmetrical in function. But in humans the cerebral hemispheres develop differently. The left hemisphere controls the right side of the body, the right hemisphere controls the left side of the body. For more than 150 years it has been understood that the function of language and language-related capabilities is mainly located in the left hemisphere. Because speech and language are so closely linked to thinking, reasoning, and the higher mental functions that set humans apart from animals, 19th-century scientists named the left hemisphere the dominant or major hemisphere. Until recently, the right hemisphere was thought to be less advanced because non-verbal, a sort of mute twin with lower-level capabilities, directed and carried along by the verbal left hemisphere.

By the 1960s scientists had revised their view of the relative capabilities of the two halves of the human brain; both hemispheres are now known to be involved in higher cognitive functions, each highly specialised for *different* modes of thinking, both highly complex. Each hemisphere in a sense perceives its own reality. The left half (controlling the right side of the body) dominates most people most of the time in our society. The left hemisphere is verbal and analytic, while the mode of the right hemisphere is non-verbal and global. The mode of processing used by the right brain is extremely rapid, complex, whole-pattern, spatial and perceptual.

The two hemispheres normally communicate with each other by means of the *corpus callosum*, a thick cable of millions of nerve fibres that cross-connects them, reconciling the two perceptions and preserving our sense of being one person, a unified being. Usually the two hemispheres work cooperatively, each taking on the particular part of a task suited to its mode of information processing. At other times they can work singly. And sometimes they are in conflict, with, in most people, the dominant verbal left hemisphere trying to do what the right half can do better or faster.

Perhaps human beings have always had some sense of the difference between the halves of our brain, because all languages contain words or customs suggesting different characteristics of the left and right sides of the body. These usually speak of hands, but because of the cross-over characteristics of hands and brain hemispheres, the terms can be understood as referring by implication to the hemispheres that control the hands. When words refer specifically to the left or right hand, they refer inferentially to the opposite brain half, since the right hand is connected to the left brain and vice versa. You will all be aware that negative connotations are usually given to the left hand - and, by inference, to the right side of the brain. For instance, the Latin for left, *sinister*, means bad or ominous. The Latin word for right is *dexter*, from which we get our idea of dextrous. This is conceptually related to the

French word *droit* for right, from which we get adroit, as opposed to *gauche*, awkward. And so on. It is essential, of course, to remember that all these terms were invented by human left-brain hemispheres - the left brain is calling the right brain bad names. And the right hemisphere/ left hand is without a language of its own to answer back.

The dualities and different characteristics of the two halves of the human brain and body, while expressed in language, are rarely experienced as conflicts on a conscious level. Nevertheless, in our society there is a tendency for the left so-called dominant hemisphere to take over and inhibit the other half. The left hemisphere analyses, abstracts, counts, marks time, plans step-by-step procedures, verbalises and makes rational statements based on logic. With the denigrated right hemisphere we use intuition, a rapid mode of information-processing. We understand metaphors, we visualise the solutions to problems, or see how things relate to each other in space. We dream in right-brain hemisphere mode, and create new combinations of ideas. Words are not required, in fact, words may fail us. When we want to describe something complicated like a spiral staircase, it is clearer and easier to gesture or draw it than to talk about it.

But the right-brain/left-handed mode in our culture is weak and generally ignored. Most of our educational system has been designed to cultivate the verbal, rational, left hemisphere. A few art classes, some music - but not classes in imaging, visualisation, perceptual or spatial skills, no courses in intuition or inventiveness...except, perhaps, in art colleges. With that exception, the emphasis of the entire culture is on left-brain skills, and increasingly so.

It might be best to think of left and right brain distinctions as a metaphor, since science, like other discourses, is historically and culturally constructed, and can therefore have only relative accuracy as being a way of describing any notional "real" world. But it seems to me an interesting and valuable metaphor, and one that I think conveys the negative attitude that informs/influences our idea of art education. Although increasingly diluted and insecure, art education has traditionally been the primary institution where right-brain traits are accorded value, and where right-brain skills are practised and perfected. This may occur under any system of modules or tutorials, but it can't be separated from an intense concentration on open-ended, non-verbal visual skills.

Oddly enough, the best arguments for expanding and emphasising the skills that have traditionally found their safest homes in art schools may come from the history of science. As I've indicated, the right brain is non-rational: it doesn't require a basis of reasonable facts. It is called intuitive and holistic because it makes irrational jumps of insight, often based on incomplete evidence. What is especially well documented in the history of Western science is that new, unexpected syntheses are often dreamt or daydreamed, that is, produced as an effect of reverie and visualisation. Niels Bohr arrived at his definitive plan of the nature of the atom by means of an archetypal dream of planets dancing round the sun. The Nobel Prize-winning chemist Kekulé's solution for the composition of benzene was a chain of molecules derived from his dreamt image of Oroborus, the ancient symbol of a serpent swallowing its own tail. These well-known examples, and many others, provide testimony of the productivity of the right brain. Such experiences may become self-reflexive, that is; the person concerned can seem to observe the operation of the mental system as it generates new ideas. Conscious access to this system characterises those individuals who are consistently productive of new ideas.

What interests me is the extent to which non-verbal, visual, non-logical thinking is emphasised in this high-level creativity. Albert Einstein wrote: "Words or language... do not seem to play any role in my mechanism of thought. The psychical entities which seem to serve as elements in thought are certain signs and more-or-less clear images which can be 'voluntarily' reproduced and combined." The 19th-century mathematician Henri Poincaré described a sudden intuition that gave him the solution to a difficult problem thus. "One evening, contrary to my custom, I drank black coffee and could not sleep. Ideas rose in crowds; I felt them collide until pairs interlocked, so to speak, making a stable combination." This strange phenomenon provided the intuition that solved the problem. "It seems in such cases that one is present at his own unconscious work, made partially perceptible to the over-excited consciousness, yet without having to change its nature. Thus we vaguely comprehend what distinguishes the two mechanisms, or, if you wish, the working methods of the two egos."

Anyone who has ever worked in art colleges knows that they are full of people who disclaim any taste or talent for abstract generalisations, logic, words. These are students whose right-brain access and ability to visualise is so strong that it has survived the educational system of our society. Other right-brain people will be found, as my examples indicate, in all fields, particularly science and mathematics; although as some scientists have recently said of scientific education, it sometimes seems as though the purpose of this education is to close down the creative functions of the right hemisphere. Speaking personally, I might trace my own development from anthropologist to artist as a history of my shift away from the dominant left-brain function toward an ever-increasing, respectful commitment to the right brain.

In my view, the art college as a site of contestation is most of all the place where right brain functions struggle, increasingly weakly, to maintain their foothold. Perhaps the recent attacks on visual education by left and right political groups alike cover up the very deep fear of the irrational and intuitive that characterises our culture. In this sense, the negative cultural placement of women artists and black artists, who have come to symbolise the denigrated aspects of our right brains, can be understood as extreme instances of this fear.

So in a very real, very serious way, I have seen your invitation to me to speak here today as an opportunity to look again and really see the British art college. Though flawed and inconsistent, it remains the only site where right-brain functions are consciously trained and utilised. If our society truly valued creativity in all fields, we would be witnessing an analysis of how art education works and an expansive intensification of its most profoundly useful aspects. Instead, we are living through a time when this special kind of education - from which all of us here have been lucky enough to benefit - is being homogenised with other kinds of education. I've nothing against mixing disciplines and fields together, far from it. I love impurity. But I'm afraid that this new mixture will totally bypass the art colleges' dedication to right-brain thinking, a dedication that could, with support and encouragement, evolve to become the core of a new kind of creativity curriculum with other disciplines organised around it. As I see it, **a truly enterprising society would explore the potential of the art college to extend its existing commitment to the conscious use of right-brain skills. A truly enterprising society would reform and transform the art college into a highly developed forum for education in the creative potentials yet to be realised in the visual, perceptual, and intuitive modes of the right brain.**

NOTES

1   The conference was **The Curriculum for Fine Art in Higher Education: The Essential Elements of Fine Art Courses in the '90s**, held at the Tate Gallery on 19th February 1993.

VII

PERIPHERAL VISION

Iain Biggs

"Don't pray for the rain to stop
Pray for good luck fishing
When the river floods."

Wendell Berry
(from **Prayers and Sayings of the Mad Farmer**)

Introduction

I have some difficulty with the set of claims implied by the prospectus for this conference. I understand that there is an emerging consensus among major art schools in north-west Europe, concerning the need for an expanded pedagogic model that gives greater emphasis to European, rather than national, contexts. This model, it is suggested, is to be based on current reassessments of our European-ness. My difficulty with this stems, I suspect, from the fact that my own dialogue with Europe has been focused by individuals from Portugal, Scandinavia and Georgia as much as from the European Community's economic heartland. This involvement with people from what economic geographers call the peripheral regions of the new Europe gives me a particular perspective on the statement that appeared in the prospectus that a European model is "an important point of reference even when it is accepted that there is a need for an art institution to reflect what Kenneth Frampton has termed 'critical regionalism'". The use of the word "even" here suggests the extent to which notions of regionalism are peripheral to this new academic "consensus".

Any marginalisation of regionalism in relation to Europe - at whatever level - has important political and cultural implications. Some economists have pointed out that the Treaty of Rome already marked a clear drift away from the Spaak Report of 1956 - which had indicated a strong regionalist and welfarist basis for the European Community - towards a free-market economy. Successive treaties have called on the Community to meet its obligation to reduce economic disparities between different regions. It has consistently failed to do so. I believe that critical regionalism has implications that go well beyond particular issues of art or architectural practice, touching on core differences as to the future cultural, economic and political orientation of Europe. Reassessments of epistemological and pedagogic models are not simply an issue for those who find they must balance the demands of art practice and academic responsibility. They are also, for example, the focus of a challenge by environmentalists, who argue that higher education is pervaded by a *"hidden* curriculum". This assumes that "human domination of nature is good, that the growth economy is natural, that all knowledge, regardless of its consequences, is equally valuable, and that material progress is our right".[1] The relationship between such a challenge and contemporary art practice is a real issue in, for example, Finland. I am unclear as to what place, if any, it might have in the pedagogic model implied by the conference prospectus. This paper explores two basic questions: "what understanding of contemporary Europe are we to assume here?" and "how do we understand ourselves, as the artist-academics making that assumption?"

Part One

Since the Coldstream Report, fine art has increasingly found it necessary to ally itself to critical theories and bodies of knowledge of various kinds. As a result there has been a tendency to neglect its function as a site for therapeutic action. However, the work of important and diverse practitioners and thinkers - for example Joseph Beuys and Julia Kristeva - requires that we consider this therapeutic function in any debate about the future of fine art.

The issue of the therapeutic function of art practice can be approached from a number of perspectives. In fine art teaching, the process of learning has two major and inter-related components. The first involves gaining knowledge and skills from others. These can be taught in reasonably systematic ways - via demonstrations, tutorials, lectures, seminars, reading and research - and can be called the *academic* component. The second component involves the transformation of what is learnt in the first, via a process of feeling and evaluation, into an informed and particular relationship between the learner, values and a developing practice. This is the *experimental* component. If we accept that the aim of the fine art course is to enable students to articulate an individually inflected vision, and that this can only be done through a process in which they constantly locate and relocate themselves - in relation both to their sense of themselves and to shared values and practices - then the experimental component is at the heart of fine art education. Where problems most frequently occur is in the way in which the student's own interests, history, identity and values can quickly become submerged by the implicit authority that underwrites the academic component. The tutor has a key therapeutic role at this point. This consists of encouraging and enabling the student to engage in a process of constant translation: between the personal and impersonal, the particular and the general, the emotional and the conceptual. This therapeutic role is paradoxical; it must both sustain the identity of the student and her or his practice, and constantly encourage their reconfiguration and change. Only if the student can internalise this therapeutic role as an aspect of practice does her or his art practice become a practice of self, as well as a material and academic practice. As such, it has a particular ethical and social dimension.

The editor of a collection of recent papers on some of the most radical aspects of post-modern thinking draws attention to the therapeutic within the debate between "ecstatics" and "philosophers of difference". One of the points linking them is the discovery, or recovery, of what she calls a "capacity for ethical action -whether this is described in terms of love, compassion, altruism or care".[2] Care - the word has the same root meaning as therapy - is here an orientation that links the social other and the other within our constantly modified sense of self. The recovery of the therapeutic in art practice has taken many forms, one of which has been what some feminists have called "the art of the particular": that which attends to the "'web of stories' which constitutes the who and what of our shared life".[3] This form of attention to our shared life escapes conceptualisation, and is best understood as a poetics.

Octavio Paz has defined poetry as "the *other* voice"; one which is "not the voice of history or of anti-history, but the voice which, in history, is always saying something different".[4] If we add theory to history in this definition, it offers us a clear sense of the position of art practice in relation to history and theory, when it is seen as therapeutic and a poetics. History and theory are, of course, important academic elements in the study of fine art.

Given the therapeutic orientation of critical regionalism, it is to be expected that Alexander Tzonis and Liane Lefaivre, who adopted the term, should describe it not as a theory or programme, but as a poetics.[5] What is important about critical regionalism in this present context - where I shall use the term in an expanded sense to suggest arts practices other than architecture, and a type of art education that might teach those practices - is that it reverses the implicit assumption upon which I take this conference to be based. That is, it *begins* with attention to specific and localised situations and experience, and only then places them in a critical relationship to wider national and international cultures.

I have pragmatic, as well as ethical, reasons for adopting such a viewpoint. Like many people working in fine art, I am employed by a regional - some might say provincial - new university. While the faculty has good links with a number of European art schools, direct contact with the professional world of the continental artist-academic is necessarily limited. In recent years it has seemed as important to establish greater interaction with local agencies and cultural groups as it has to expand our European connections. One reason for this has been my concern that financial cuts would increasingly drive us into a provincial relationship to major metropolitan centres, inevitably more favoured by the mandarin curatorial culture. The alternative to this enforced drift towards provincialism has been to involve ourselves in educational and cultural policies that have a self-consciously regionalist perspective.

This regionalist orientation is in no sense a move away from teaching within a European perspective. However, it does involve a more selective attitude to art practices that are aimed at an international audience, and greater attention to locally inflected and oriented practices - including public and community arts. Like environmentalists, we are beginning to place a greater emphasis on "thinking globally, acting locally". What critical regionalism has to offer us is a perspective that stresses concern with the recreation and cultivation of a locally-rooted sense of culture; one which, however, does not play into the hands of nostalgia and kitsch. It also supports practices which are both fully contemporary and able to draw on traditional sources. Above all, it encourages practitioners to place themselves in a therapeutic relationship to communities, to look to foster local characteristics and a particularised sense of identity; while being open to, and selectively drawing on, ideas, forms and images from other sources and cultures. In short, critical regionalism provides a focus, in the terms defined earlier, for a shift of emphasis from the generalised academic bias current in much art education towards a particular and experimental bias, with a consciously therapeutic and social dimension.

This orientation also has a broader political and cultural aspect. The region in which I work has been badly hit by recession and declining industry. Today the local Health Authority, with whom we are increasingly involved, is the largest single employer in the region. The phrase "two Europes" once referred to the split between East and West. More and more it comes to refer to the division between *core* and *peripheral* economic regions.[6] A number of regions in Britain are increasingly drifting from the first towards the second category, largely as a result of the rise of a post-industrial economy. As yet the political and social perspectives to which critical regionalism relates are underdeveloped in Britain, where "traditional perceptions of regions, as static closed entities corresponding to similarly invariant, insular groups" linger on.[7] Yet it is within this broader context that critical regionalism is ultimately most important. Critical regionalism offers the basis for an alternative cultural approach and educational orientation, which neither nationalist nor internationalist priorities can easily render marginal or provincial. Its orientation relates to alternative perspectives such as environmentalism, and does not turn its back on the cultural life of regions that are currently economically peripheral.

Attention is increasingly being directed to the social and philosophical foundations of the European psychoanalytic and psychotherapeutic traditions, and to their parallels and interaction with art practice and with theory. As a result I believe our understanding of the cultural and social dimensions of the therapeutic will change. That change should encourage at least some art schools to give renewed attention to the therapeutic functions of art. I believe this can best be done within a regionalist context, one that is both critical and therapeutic. However, this development is likely to meet strong resistance in various quarters, because it will challenge the epistemological and pedagogic basis of much current fine art teaching. It will also challenge the ways in which our culture is currently professionalised and institutionalised on the basis of a particular set of economic and political priorities.

Having indicated my general concerns, I will now turn to more particular issues. I shall look first at some aspects of professionalism as they relate to the European economic context, and then at the relationship between these and what is excluded from a recent discussion of possible models for the art academy.

Part Two

Two current attitudes to professionalism can be crudely polarised as follows. Professionalism can be understood positively as the sum of knowledges and skills - historical, cultural, critical, promotional and so on - necessary to support economically successful art practice. It can also be understood negatively, in the context of the post-war professionalisation of visual culture; something brought about by investment in specialist knowledges as a basis for professional authority, and part of an overarching and systematic discourse of control.[8] The professionalism of the contemporary artist-academic will include aspects that correspond to *both* of these understandings. This ambiguous and perhaps paradoxical situation, that of contradictory orientations, corresponds to models of human existence offered us by some contemporary psychologies that stress our innate diversity, "both among individuals and *within each individual*".[9] I want to examine the ambivalence of our sense of professionalism in this psychological context.

Susan Hiller has offered a view of the artist in relation to art education that appeals strongly to many people. It focuses on "doing art" as something quite specific, something to be defended from what she describes as a continual "slide from *practice* to *theory*, from particular *experiences* to generalised *abstractions*, from the *dream* to the *word*, from *art* to *education*".[10] She also calls into question the way in which fine art courses are used to validate notions of professionalism. She argues that this masks a more fundamental priority, that of contesting the unequal relationship in society between dominant systems of control, and more intuitive and irrational modes of thinking - including visual thinking. She calls for an art college that is a specialist site for the education "of the visual, perceptual and intuitive modes of the right brain". Hiller's argument is in some respects a strong one, powerfully supported by work done by agencies like the Arts Dyslexia Trust, which are involved in looking at the relationship between creative thinking and the bias within dominant forms of current education.[11] Although I share some of Hiller's priorities, I believe that they should be framed in another way. As the philosopher Geraldine Finn has cogently observed, we are all in actuality *"always both more and less than the categories which name and divide us"*[emphasis mine].[12] It seems to me more productive to attend to this area of *"more and less"*, rather than to set art practice, the particular and the dream against education, the general and the word. What is critical here is the extent of our ability constantly to negotiate and renegotiate our relationship to these concerns; to focus more attention on the "experimental" rather than the "academic" approach. What often prevents us from doing so is our own notion of professionalism. This is heavily conditioned by our identification, either with the authority generated by theory, or with the priorities of the administered world of the academy. In short, we need to resist the reduction of our complex and ambivalent lived experience to a professional category. It is the general failure of the artist-academic to do this that has resulted in the situation indicated by Adorno's observation that "whoever speaks of culture speaks of administration, whether it is his intention or not".[13] The category is, of course, the basis of all administrative systems. We can understand something of how we reduce ourselves to categories of professionalism by looking both at our relationship to the economic concerns of the administered world of the academy, and at the contemporary emphasis on the authority of theory.

In 1993 student applications through ADAR rose by thirty per cent to about 33,000, while Department of Education funding to art and design courses dropped - also by thirty per cent.[14] This situation is specific to Britain. However, these figures tell us little of the larger pattern of events, unless they are seen as part of a change that includes the centralisation of higher education and the shift towards a research, rather than educational, culture. It is at this level that all these changes come to reflect the new role of the university in the European post-industrial economic order. In that order the university becomes a key growth point in the production of theoretical knowledge, information processing, the development and control of high technology and, most critically, the production of systems of assessment and control central to all these activities.[15] British higher education has been recontextualised as a service industry, subject like any other to market forces, quality assurance and control, and "enlightened" government intervention. As a result a growing number of people are questioning whether our universities as institutions now have "the capacity to meet a growing crisis that is not only ecological and technological, but ultimately educational and moral".[16]

Art practice, carried out within the growing sphere of influence of the university and its values, is now reconceptualised as research. As a result it becomes subject to new controls and values. To survive in the university, the artist-academic must increasingly match the categories and priorities that research ratings reward. That is, he or she is under growing pressure to move from an "experimental" to an "academic" bias in her or his practice, academic in the sense already indicated. Institutions are investing heavily in the technologies of information, for example in the sophisticated electronic workstations upon which scholarship is now increasingly dependent. This in turn is redefining the nature of research and the role of the universities. The obvious price of all this is paid in Britain by students, whose studies are increasingly underfunded. Ever larger numbers are now leaving courses, as a result of economic hardship and diminished academic and pastoral support. The results of both the reconceptualisation of practice as research, and the academic shift to an information culture, are the same: they bring educational priorities into line with those of the European Community as a ***post-industrial economic power***. Both educational and Community policies increasingly privilege a research orientation over basic educational and welfare needs. In both cases the free-market approach is winning out over the social welfarist perspective. A specific example would be the way in which Community regional, educational and social funds are kept at such a level as to be quite unable to meet the needs for which they were established, while European multi-nationals are assisted to compete with the United States and East Asia through technological research funds.

In this situation we may wish to ask to what extent any move towards academic multi-nationalism is simply a further attempt to match the policies of post-industrial European economics. To answer this we would need to determine whether the emphasis is largely on the north-west - what economic geographers call the "fortress" of the European economy - and on cities like Barcelona that are central to the post-industrial core regions.[17] Whatever the answer, it is very clear that many of the issues that face us are now determined to a greater or lesser extent by economic rather than cultural or educational concerns and priorities. As a result our professionalism is constantly at risk of becoming identified with particular administrative and economically determined categories, which increasingly tend to deny the experimental or therapeutic aspects of art practice. Consequently there is already a growing category of people who might be described as the "new European professionals". While we cannot ignore or avoid the economic dimension of the new post-industrial Europe, it does seem to me important that our practice remains in a critical and therapeutic relation to that dimension and the values that go with it - if only in so far as we wish to articulate a critical and regionalist perspective.

Practice can be frozen into a fixed category when it identifies too closely with the authority of theory. Current explorations of the role of theory in psychotherapeutic practices have much to teach us in this respect. Experimentally oriented art practice, in the sense I have defined, requires conditions that include elements of play, insecurity, and respect for, and openness to, what is other - both in ourselves and socially. Too great a fascination or identification with theory can prevent experimental practice - if by theory we understand any internally consistent and authoritative perspective. Academic success increasingly depends on the research returns generated by an intellectual investment in specialist knowledge. This in turn creates a vested interest in expanding the field of concern to which that specialist knowledge can be applied. Like the financial world, the academic world has learnt that "corporate raiding" is a quicker and more productive means of getting a high return, in terms of research, than the slower and more laborious process of original work. Experimental art practices are almost by definition open-ended, plural in their sources and prospective in their outcomes. In short, they tend to be under-theorised. They are thus the ideal target for the academic "corporate raider". As Susan Hiller suggests, art practices of this sort are easily treated as "raw material for other discourses, as the speech of the native is appropriated by the anthropologist, or the dream of the patient is 'written up' by the therapist".[18] As a result of this situation, there is a very strong temptation for artists to "do a deal" with the academic corporate raider, borrowing the support of theoretical discourses in return for establishing a more authoritative place for practice in the academy. The price of this is, however, the gradual shift in emphasis from the experimental to the academic in art practice, since the identity of both artist and practice becomes increasingly inseparable from the academic priorities of the discourse to which it is related.

If we wish to protect the experimental, educational and therapeutic aspects of art practice as I have defined them, then we have to enter wider debates about the epistemological and pedagogic basis of the academy *as a whole*. In particular, we need to distinguish between the ways in which different disciplines *function* in relation to each other. Something of what is involved in this can be indicated by trying to distinguish "combative" from "therapeutic" approaches to interdisciplinary exchange and activity.

Combative approaches may be understood in the context of the psychological view that fascination with theory can be seen in a psychologically negative light as a defence against psychosis and death; that is to say, against the possibility of any dissolution and transformation of a fixed and authoritative sense of self. *It is, of course, just this possibility of transformation within experimental art practice that gives it a therapeutic dimension*. Combative approaches or practices within the university can thus be linked to a sense of chronic individualism or narcissism, where the identity of the artist or academic becomes dependent on, and inseparable from her, or his sense of professionalism. This results in what might be called *professional narcissism*.[19] Professional narcissists invest emotionally in specialist knowledge to gain a privileged place in the social sphere, upon which their survival as narcissists depends. Such people are often identified by obsessive concern with their professional peer group, preoccupation with placings within that group, and by zealous protection and promotion of its specialist discursive practices and privileges.

The anthropologist David Napier has described such people as exemplary models of "a self working hard at being its own worst enemy". They focus on their identity as artists or academics to the exclusion of all other "activities which define a person's connectedness and ontological status".[20] Conversations with those who teach fine art graduates on postgraduate art therapy courses confirm that art schools regularly produce just such people.

In contrast to the combative approach, therapeutic approaches are rooted in an ethical concern with open-ended relationships, which can be characterised *as care or respect for the other*. It is important to keep in mind, however, that this other is always both a component of our own psychic world, and of the shared or social world. Therapeutic approaches may also be critical, but they hold to an ethical orientation by which they constantly relativise and question their own position, in order to open to the larger needs and experience of the shared world. They point to a form of interdisciplinary relationship that is not combative, but rooted in a relationship of mutual and experimental learning.

At present a very real tension exists between tendencies towards these two conflicting approaches within the academy. The pressure to generate high personal research profiles, together with rapid change and economic recession, may well reinforce the tendency towards professional narcissism. Unless we attend to the problem of combative practices, we may well find ourselves in a situation like that increasingly apparent in the United States, where "grand narcissistic fantasies" are "in many instances socially adaptive".[21]

Increasingly the space of play in psychotherapy appears to be identical with the space of the poetic imagination, itself the common ground between experimental aspects of art and education. Both seek "keener interactive experience" understood in terms of "interpretation and mediation... between contexts".[22] This common experimental ground is also central to critical regionalism, in terms of its desire to promote what Jerome Bruner calls "a democracy of experience" and a "forum of possible worlds".[23] These considerations seem to me to take us beyond professionalism as we usually understand it, and into a realm that certain French thinkers have discussed in terms of a new form of *amateurism*. This new amateurism is an attitude that, regardless of the particular disciplines in which the practitioner may be involved, adopts an approach based on the understanding that, potentially, nothing is insignificant in terms of the experimental reconstitution of subjectivity.

Miroslav Holub, who is both a poet and a scientist, distinguishes between those two roles by claiming that the former "is based on the *binding inadequacy* of its means"; while the latter "insists on the *adequacy*, or at least the temporary adequacy, of its means".[24] It has been argued that professionalised academic culture depends upon a single fundamental assumption: that it can speak from "a position of mastery" over the "texts" with which it concerns itself. To obtain such a position of mastery demands, as Jane Gallop puts it, that one "constantly cover one's inevitable inadequacy in order to have the right to speak".[25] The link between this adequacy of professionalised academic mastery and the authority of instrumental science - a shared emphasis on authority derived from the primacy of internally consistent methodologies - is highly suggestive. I would argue that it is this conflict - between an academy based on the *combative* forms of academic mastery and one based on therapeutic approaches that can accept and value "inevitable inadequacy" - that should be at the heart of the current pedagogic debate.

To see the orientation of the artist-academic as critically "amateur" reflects Julia Kristeva's view of the artist as someone having the ability constantly to problematise and relativise their practice as inadequate; "as though it were a living system that lives only on condition of being open to the other".[26] Holub indicates the practical implications of this by asking why we attach such importance to our professional identity when, as he puts it: "95 per cent of our time we are really secretaries, telephonists, passers-by, carpenters, plumbers, privileged and underprivileged citizens, waiting patrons, applicants, household maids, clerks, commuters, offenders, listeners, drivers, runners, patients, losers, subjects and shadows?"[27] Such an acknowledgement of our plurality of roles would mean that we would have to be more open about our constant shift between, for example, "person presumed to know" and "person not in command". It is this that points to a radical democratisation in education, one that seeks to promote a genuine cultural democracy, rather than becoming simply the instrument of national or international programmes. Cultural democracy constitutes a tradition that we should surely seek to perpetuate. It is unfettered by geographic and economic demarcations, yet must always be interpreted in terms that are particular to local or regional circumstances.

Part Three

Lucio Pozzi has argued that we are now facing the unprecedented task of going beyond both the "regressive academy of conservatism" and the "progressive academy of transgression".[28] This seems to me to be essentially correct. However, I know of no account of fine art education in this country on which a discussion along these lines could be based. By using an account that is perhaps neither authoritative nor representative, I hope nonetheless to reflect on issues that relate to our current educational practice. In 1992 David Sweet produced a paper entitled **Towards a Militant Academy**.[29] This offers an argument for an approach that can reasonably be described as conservative, nationalistic and provincial. I would argue that it is conservative, rather than traditional, not simply because it effectively ignores all media other than painting, sculpture and print; but also because it fails to locate those traditional media in terms of values and concerns that constitute a living tradition. It is nationalistic in ignoring both Europe and the existence of distinctive postgraduate courses developed in Wales, Northern Ireland, north-east England and Scotland. It is provincial in its adoption of a single, vertical and one-way educational model, where London colleges become the only and inevitable focus for thinking about art education. In short, I believe that Sweet's "Militant Academy" corresponds fairly closely to Pozzi's notion of a "regressive academy of conservatism".

Sweet's paper reduces all debate about the art academy to a set of choices between four student types, where each is seen as "the imaginary entity those who design courses have in mind as the ideal recipient of the educational package offered".[30] The four colleges upon whom the types are based are the Royal Academy Schools, the Royal College of Art, the Slade School of Fine Art and Goldsmiths' College. Sweet's argument is specifically directed against the last three models, and in terms that he would no doubt see as consistent with Pozzi's notion of the "progressive academy of transgression". Sweet sees these three models as collectively responsible for the creation of an approach to art practice and education that results in an unholy alliance of opportunistic professionalism and inappropriate emphasis on theoretical study. I have already discussed similar concerns, although on a very different basis, and would see them as compatible with Pozzi's second characterisation. I would not, however, *necessarily* identify this characterisation with the colleges Sweet identifies.

It should be clear that I am not concerned here with David Sweet's specific argument for a Militant Academy, some of which seems to me constructive. What concerns me is the reductive context within which that argument is framed. While I am fairly certain that the majority of fine art staff would reject the greater part of his paper's specific argument, I doubt that they would necessarily question its parameters, beyond some concern about the exclusion of Europe. I am interested in what those parameters exclude because of what this may tell us about preoccupations and priorities in fine art. At the very least, the paper excludes four areas of postgraduate study that require a degree in fine art or equivalent. One is that of social and public practices of art, as developed by courses such as Duncan of Jordanstone's MFA in Public Art and Design. Another is the broad spectrum of educational concern, from the University of Sussex's Language, the Arts and Education to standard postgraduate courses in art and design education. A third area is that of courses related to art therapy, particularly the postgraduate training diplomas. A fourth area is one now being developed, in women's art practice. I suspect that a good many fine art staff still either ignore these areas or see them as peripheral; as the concern of students too lacking in ambition to aim for what is still seen as the pinnacle of fine art study -a place at a London postgraduate college. Ironically, however, it might be that a student's interest in the public, educational, therapeutic and/or feminist contexts of art practice, would most obviously demonstrate an understanding of the therapeutic, as I have used the term here.

I am not arguing that we should be preparing undergraduate students to go on to vocational postgraduate courses. The criticism of vocationalism in British art education - often made by continental academics - is beside the point here. On the contrary, I am arguing that these contexts relate directly to our lived experience of culture in its most immediate sense - that is, as *"the way we do things here"*, in this specific situation, in terms of the values and principles that underlie our day-to-day enterprises and inform our normal activities.[31] It is for this reason that public, educational, therapeutic and feminist contexts are important to any genuinely experimentally oriented fine art practice.

In 1970, Octavio Paz wrote a powerful critique of the view of art that sees value as inseparable from categories "of history, progress and modernity". In this critique he identifies a growing need for at least two new - or perhaps very old - understandings of art. The first he links to fiesta or carnival: an art that satisfies our need for "collective rites". The second he links to a "no less imperative need" for "solitary meditation and contemplation"; one that we might now see in terms of growing post-secular tendencies within European society.[32] By 1984 Umberto Eco had developed a notion of carnival that has been of considerable importance. This can be related to attitudes and practices that were already being developed by artists working right on the edge of fine art practice, or else within the context of community arts. One outcome of all this is that East London University can celebrate the arts of carnival, in conjunction with local schools and the community at large. In 1985

Brandon Taylor argued, within a socialist conception of contemporary art, for the need to respect certain modernist art practices in the context of therapeutic insights. He argued that "progress" can be understood within that context as part of "a search for meaning rather than a utopian plan".[33] An alternative but related revisioning of aspects of early modern practice has been suggested by Martha Kapos in relation to the work of Ken Kiff.[34] These examples suggest a rich context for a therapeutic understanding of revised modern practice, fruitful in that which are denied to the conservatism of the Militant Academy.

If we are to adopt a more open and therapeutic view of the function of art education we must find space for a wide range of approaches, some rooted in traditional media and some not. While the nature and content of the academic elements of particular courses will, in such circumstances, need to differ, the commitment to the experimental element should be constant. A major stumbling block to this is the question of the relationship of practice to theory. Sweet's Militant Academy assumes a student concerned with "the unmediated activities of making art".[35] Susan Hiller is also critical of anything that takes the student away from "'doing' art". It seems to me that in both cases something vital gets forgotten.

A recent NAFAE seminar on the relation of practice to theory concluded that many, perhaps most, fine art students arrive on undergraduate courses with views about their practice that derive from particular theories of art - often related to expression - but that they hold these views unconsciously or uncritically. Those who dismiss theory as having no place within the fine art curriculum do not produce "theory-free" students, even when they seek to save them from the tyrannies of inappropriate verbal analysis and iconophobia. We are in reality saved from these only by better, more rigorous, yet therapeutically oriented approaches to the functions of theory. Good theory should surely free us into deeper and more inclusive forms of experience and understanding, rather than binding us to, or proscribing, particular practices and attitudes.

If theory is to be in some sense constantly both learnt and then dispensed with, it must first have been properly understood and consciously acknowledged. All art practice is conducted on the basis of what has been transmitted and taught, at least as soon as it develops beyond a very rudimentary stage. Paradoxically, experimental practice involves something like a constant and creative "forgetting", or perhaps a constant acknowledgement of lack or inadequacy, which allows what has been transmitted or taught continually to be partially dissolved or reconfigured by particular concerns and values. Only on this basis can we enter new relationships and configurations of self and other, in a shared yet particular polyphony of voices and dreams. Precisely such art practice *would* make possible the aspirations of critical regionalism to a "democracy of experience" and a "forum of possible worlds" - some of which will of course be those of European culture, variously understood.

At the beginning of this paper I raised two questions, about our understanding of contemporary Europe and our understanding of ourselves. I believe the first question is finally subsumed into the second. In short, the key issue is not our relationship to Europe but our understanding of ourselves - as Europeans but also as both more and less than Europeans. I do not believe that we should allow ourselves to become categorised as professional artist-academics of the new Europe. We need a broader and more open approach and other, ethical priorities. There is plenty of evidence to suggest that what we call the person or self has, in fact, never been quite the unified and monolithic entity recent thinking has been so keen to deconstruct. What Andrew Samuels calls the "decentered subject, an actor playing many roles in many scripts, characterised by luck, somewhat faded as well as jaded, jerky, marginalised, alienated, split, guilty, empty" - even "imaginary" - has been around far longer than is usually acknowledged.[36] It is for reflecting on, and even celebrating, this consistently inconsistent and plural person that artists have always fallen foul of the dogmas and absolutes of those who claim authority on the basis of mastery of religious, aesthetic, social, historical, theoretical, economic or political positions. This paper is addressed to this decentered, plural person that we all are, but may refuse to acknowledge in the name of professionalism; the person who "makes and is made by the world in a ceaseless generative struggle".[37] I believe that this person is critically both more and less than a new European; indeed, both more - and no doubt also less - than a professional artist-academic. I trust we can keep it that way.

NOTES

1   David Orr, **Schools for the Twenty-First Century**, in **Resurgence** (September - October 1993, No. 160, Schumacher Society, Hartland, Devon, UK), p. 17.

2   Philippa Berry, introduction to P. Berry and A. Wernick, eds., **Shadow of Spirit: Postmodernism and Religion** (Routledge, UK, 1992), p. 5.

3   Seyla Benhahib, introduction to **Situating the Self**, (Polity Press, Cambridge, 1992).

4   Octavio Paz, **Selected Poems** (Penguin, UK, 1979), p. 13.

5   Alexander Tzonis and Liane Lefaivre, **Why Critical Regionalism Today?**, in **A&U** (May 1990, Volume 236, Japanese Architecture Company, Tokyo), p. 25.

6   On this see Jeffrey Anderson, who argues that "throughout the post-war era...most West European states have encompassed two nations, one prosperous, the other poor". Jeffrey J. Anderson, **The Territorial Imperative** (Cambridge University Press, 1992), p. 1. A full discussion of the relationship between core and periphery economic regions is found in Andrew H.Dawson, **A Geography of European Integration** (Belhaven Press, New York and London 1993).

7   Alexander Tzonis and Liane Lefaivre, op. cit.

8   See for example Andrew Brighton, **Resurrection of the Image**, in **Art & Design**, (Volume 4, No. 9/10, VCH Publishers (UK) Ltd, Cambridge), pp. 61-62.

9   James Hillman, **Archetypal Psychology: A Brief Account** (Spring Publications Inc., Dallas, 1983), p. 32.

10 Susan Hiller, **An Artist Looks at Art Education**, in **The Curriculum for Fine Art in Higher Education in the nineties**.(Wimbledon School of Art and The Tate Gallery, London, 1993), p. 43. Reprinted in this book as Chapter VII.

11 See for example Thomas G. West, **In the Mind's Eye** (Prometheus Books, Buffalo, New York, 1991).

12 Geraldine Finn, **The politics of spirituality: the spirituality of politics,** in P. Berry and A.Wernick eds., **Shadows of Spirit: Postmodernism and Religion** (Routledge, UK, 1992), p. 113.

13 Theodor W. Adorno, **Culture and Administration**, in J.M. Bernstein, ed., **The Culture Industry** (Routledge, UK, 1991), p. 93.

14 Jilly Welch, **Crash Course** in **Design Week** (8th October, 1993), p. 17.

15 Albert Borgmann, **Crossing the Postmodern Divide** (University of Chicago Press, USA, 1992), p. 60-61.

16 David Orr, op. cit., p. 17.

17 Andrew H. Dawson, op. cit., p. 44.

18 Susan Hiller, op. cit. P.43.

19 This paper has drawn on a range of works relating to what is here described as "narcissism" or "professional narcissism". The most important are: i) Stephen Bann, **The True Vine** (Cambridge University Press, 1989). ii) Donald Kuspit, **The Cult of the Avant-garde Artist** (Cambridge University Press, 1993). iii) David A. Napier, **Foreign Bodies: Performance, Art and Symbolic Anthropology** (University of California Press, 1992).

20 David A.Napier, op. cit., p. 22-23.

21 Brandon Taylor, **Modernism, Post-Modernism, Realism** (Winchester School of Art Press, UK, 1987), p. 120.

22 Katy Macleod, **Pedagogy and the Poetic: a moment of recognition,** a paper delivered at the **Anti Conference** organised

by Griselda Pollock and held at Leeds University in September 1993.

23 Alexander Tzonis and Liane Lefaivre, op. cit.

24 Miroslav Holub, **Poetry and Science**, in David Young, ed., **The Dimension of the Present Moment and Other Essays.**(Faber and Faber, London, 1990), p. 132.

25 Jane Gallop, **Reading Lacan** extract reprinted in R. Ferguson, W. Olander, M.Tucker and F. Fiss eds., **Discourses: Conversations in Postmodern Art and Culture**. (MIT Press, Cambridge Mass., USA), pp. 446-447.

26 Julia Kristeva, quoted in John Lechte, **Julia Kristeva** (Routledge, UK, 1990), p. 215.

27 Miroslav Holub, op. cit., p. 145.

28 Lucio Pozzi, **Creative Shadows** in K. Barnaby and P. d'Acierno, eds., **C.G.Jung and the Humanities**. (Routledge, UK, 1990), p. 150.

29 David Sweet, **Towards a Militant Academy** (Manchester Polytechnic, 1992).

30 *Ibid*. p. 1.

31 Ellen Noonan, **Tradition in Training**, in Laurence Spurling, ed., **From the Words of My Mouth** (Routledge, UK, 1993), p. 22.

32 Octavio Paz, **Convergences** (Bloomsbury, London, 1987), pp. 269-278.

33 Brandon Taylor, op. cit., p. 120.

34 Martha Kapos, **Illuminating Images**, in **Ken Kiff: Painting 1965-1985** (Arts Council of Great Britain, 1986), pp. 35-43.

35 David Sweet, op. cit., p. 5.

36 Andrew Samuels, **The Political Psyche** (Routledge, UK, 1993), p. 203.

37 *Ibid*. p. 204.

VIII

THE FRANKFURT STÄDELSCHULE

Kasper König

I have decided to speak about my experience and about my ideas of what an art school can be. I hope it will present a model, but it may not be a model that is applicable to you.

Just to tell you a little about myself. I have been teaching for roughly ten years. I applied for a professorship in Düsseldorf after I had been in Nova Scotia for four years, at the Nova Scotia College of Art and Design, where I started a University Press. I used my time in Nova Scotia to have an education at an art school whilst being paid as a teacher responsible for the Press. Now my relationship to art schools is no longer as selfish as it perhaps once was. However, I maintain a certain kind of independence to undertake other projects. Being responsible for, and taking very seriously, the daily business of the art school and at the same time doing things that are not directly related does not make me schizophrenic. For a very long time I have been living and working in the context of art; I am not an artist but I follow very much what artists do. I try to define my own contribution and try to objectify it in some way. I hope that people who relate their activity to art can be judged in a similar way to artists. Undue compromises are not acceptable; one should not have a controlled overview. Yet one should not be too offhand. In other words I am not without experience, having had a relationship with art in a number of different roles.

I was asked to make a brief synopsis of what I wanted to say and it is: art would go on even if there were no art schools. That this definitely is so I find rather productive because I think it is very good to have fine art academies that are free to redefine their functions all the time. Their basic purpose, I think, is to propose questions about the function and autonomy of art; that is, to deal with the past, and the future, being in the present. Obviously it would be a kind of undue privilege if the people who work in an art school, and the students, were not responsible towards one another. Not necessarily so much in a social sense, more in the articulation of aesthetic positions. This does not mean, or imply, necessarily, a kind of philosophy of how art should be considered in general, but relates specifically to one particular institution.

I guess I stand very much for the "mandarin curatorial culture", mentioned earlier by Iain Biggs, or even for multi-nationalism. Yet I do not see myself so much as an official, even though I have assumed a very official role, being the Rector, the Head, of the particular school where I am teaching now, the Städelschule. However, we have an extremely basic democratic constitution; that is, all students and professors decide on the future content of the teaching, and who is going to don the faculty hats. This is very much the result of a particular historical situation. It stems from the trauma of the Second World War when, under the Nazi regime, art was used very much from a populist point of view. Contemporary art, avant-garde art, was used to denounce any kind of spiritual or intellectual articulation, against nationhood and so on. So in West Germany after the war art and the freedom of art was re-established, actually within the constitution after the war. This had a kind of shadow side to it, because contemporary art as such was sanctioned almost in a religious way, and differentiation was not really possible. Modern art was considered to be progressive, open, a kind of civil virtue. So-called avant-garde artists, even though they may have only been avant-garde in the regional sense, and maybe only for two or three seasons, somehow made a name for themselves and then became professors in art schools. As a result there developed a kind of status quo, and this is the negative side of these institutions. However, there is more or less a liberal flow of art schools and these schools are very much defined by how many students apply and since they do not have to pay for their tuition you get a lot of students who have very specific reasons why they want to apply to a certain school. Reputations take six or seven years to spread and by the time a school gets a good reputation the momentum has already gone elsewhere.

Art academies are basically 19th-century institutions. Most of them are products of the Enlightenment of the ruling classes, who tried to prove that they were going along with the changing times. There is also a definite regional momentum that is part of German history; it is important to remember that German history has been negatively defined because of the First World War and then the Second World War. You know, Auschwitz. One does not see so easily the positive momentum that exits which is very much related to decentralisation and linked to a competitiveness between cities, and city states, and local cultures that are very much connected to the language and cultural developments.

At our school we are much more concerned about art than about culture. I find it helpful to refer to a remark of Sigmund Freud, who said that art is the enemy of culture, that culture is the relationship between young and old, foreigners and locals, the matter of the knife and fork of civilisation. While art obviously exists within culture, it is also an antidote to culture. Therefore, at many of the more interesting schools, we don't even talk about culture as such, but about particular artists who are identifiable with certain aspects within the visual arts, yet without linking them to defined categories, as signature artists have defined paintings and graphics and so on and so on. We got rid of all the departmental categories so that we can appoint and hire people as guest professors according to what we feel is absolutely necessary at a particular time. This allows us to offer opposite points of view so that students cannot really align themselves with a fixed position. Falling in between these categories, they are forced to deal with their own traumatic situation and are not allowed to follow a signature artist. We also try to overcome the "star" system which is very much built into the art system and can create a terrible atmosphere within a school, when there are certain artists who are very successful, for whatever reason, at a certain time, and others who are not but who may be producing more substantial work. These factors can easily be misused as a motive for avoiding teaching students or, conversely, for overdirecting their studies. So again I don't think it is really possible to devise a model. I also believe that many of those models that are referred to as models, such as the Bauhaus, are a myth. If you look behind them, they are not true models. They were basically known for the artists who were teaching there together, and for a few assistants who carried out some of their utopian momentum - the new Bauhaus in Chicago, for instance or the Black Mountain College, and so on. However, such models are very much locked into their political and historical situation and the Bauhaus would have died anyway, although there is a basis on which one can easily create a wonderful myth.

We continuously pose to our students the question: have you come to an art school because you have a presupposed idea of what art is, which is rather ridiculous? It might be a very good place in which to find out about yourself and to learn how to live a fulfilled life. If you don't become an artist that does not mean that you have failed in life. We are dealing with a kind of value system that society insists on; the art world and the artist play a role that society likes to rely on and this is a reality to be dealt with.

On the other hand, we could try to devalue this and create new kinds of role models, which ultimately do not have application within social and political reality. What I am talking about may sound a little naïve to you and it does have a sort of luxurious dilettantish air. But I feel that an art school is only as good as the definitions of what art can be, or does not have to be, which it poses. Ultimately it should be a place in which to work against brainwashing. This anti-brainwashing club or place obviously works best when it fulfils certain kinds of possibilities: it should have a good library; it should have a good cafeteria; it should be open, ideally, for at least eighteen hours a day. It should have good workshops. It is necessary to help students to get an overview and an idea of their desires and how they could be fulfilled. To ask them if they have desires, how they can define them and if they want them to be fulfilled.

There is a traditional thesis that if desires or wishes are strong enough then technical ideas of how to make will come by themselves; that is, true intensity produces innovation. Now this is obviously a very dangerous idea because it uses modernism and the avant-garde as a role model, whereas conditions today are completely different. We insist that all the students study art history. They have to study it for at least four terms and they have to take a course and receive credits for it. It is not easy to find art historians who are willing to teach art history not just within their speciality, but looking comprehensively at this mirror to the present. The same goes for teaching courses in philosophy that not only tackle aesthetics but also give a general overview of philosophy. This need is partly due to the fact that many of the students who apply to us do not necessarily have the basic education that one would expect them to have.

Approximately eight hundred students apply each year. We accept between thirty and fifty for one week, during which they sit a sort of extensive examination that is not too authoritarian but is very thorough. They write an essay; they do a life drawing; they pick a picture postcard, (one from some 2000) and they explain why they picked that particular one. We talk to them about which movies they have seen recently, and which music they like best. Eventually we might take ten or fifteen of these students. It may sound like a highly elitist selection process. When these students are accepted they are pretty much left alone. We got rid of the foundation course (the German word for it is fore-course, which is a sort of Bauhaus invention) for various reasons; the two artists who were in charge of this course were doing such a great job that they were exhausted because they continued being tutors for students in their subsequent years. Students who had a problem or a crisis would call them at four o'clock in the morning. So we simply said these two artists are overburdened and we got rid of the course, agreeing that students could join the professors' classes directly. We scrapped this introductory course about four years ago yet we are now seriously discussing whether to re-establish it. It is interesting, having talked to colleagues, to discover that this has happened in many schools. We plan thoroughly certain programmes that are necessary at a particular time, and then they become institutionalised and we get rid of them - and then under different conditions they are started again. I think this is absolutely acceptable. I doubt greatly that one could design an overall strategy for an art school; I believe it has a lot to do with the particular necessities, and with the precedents, that an art school has established. To me, continuity is the most important aspect and we continuously argue that we should do this or should do that because we can be sure that the school will still be around in the next twenty or thirty years when most of us who are presently involved will not be with it any more.

We have professors offering particular classes and these artists must accept a student into a class. We will never accept students unless one of our colleagues has said: "Yes, I will be happy to have him or her in my class." Of course, they can change classes. We have a lot of guest professors and a lot of fluctuations. Many of the students, who usually stay three or four years at the school, ultimately have to lose their identification with the school; they have to overcome it. But then, a couple of years after leaving they might still have a kind of loose relationship to it. So the school is, paradoxically, a way to overcome the school. Nevertheless, I believe that these institutions, since they have survived, should exist and that they should be as independent as possible - but also that they should not take themselves too seriously.

The role I am presently fulfilling is to be rather provocative to my various colleagues, some of whom are very successful as artists and some of whom are extremely orthodox, especially some of those who have a genuine avant-garde stance. Artistic conflicts have to be worked through and the attitudes the teachers use to deal with the students are extremely important. Conflicts of aesthetic difference have to be worked out in front of the students without being, in a personal way, antagonistic. I consider it is very important for students to follow these differences. When we have a discussion about the new media (which are very expensive, when computer-generated images that require mathematicians, physicists and computer specialists are being produced) some argue that it is more important to know how to make a sandwich than how to work with a computer. The other side of the argument says, okay, the most basic material is a pencil and a piece of paper and the computer and all this machinery is nothing but the pencil. It happens to be a million times more expensive but just because it is so much more expensive is no reason to devalue it, it is an everyday tool and it should be available. These contradictions have to be worked through and the fact is that whatever new media come into being the previous ones just redefine themselves and continue to exist. So I believe it is important to have a Chair of Photography, and a Chair of Printing, so that the students understand the basic culture of etchings and drypoint and lithography and so on because cultural history is also part of our own history. Devaluing the computer and grappling with the computer head-on, can both be done without being nostalgic. This is basically what makes art schools important and justifiable to taxpayers. Even though I myself am quite involved in organising exhibitions and editing books I have never felt it necessary or right to question the mechanisms of the art world in an art school. I find it is completely unnecessary to tell students how to fill out a tax form should they become artists, how to present a portfolio in order to get themselves into exhibitions and so on. I believe the commercialisation of art colleges, them streamlining into the art world of today, is very questionable because by the time students have learnt the ropes things are changing anyway; and it is ultimately the responsibility of the artist to change the structure, to make demands, to make the structure adopt their intellectual changes.

We are trying to involve more and more outside people, - such as anthropologists or, once in a while, scientists - who talk about their work and their own thinking, and they are pleased and very glad to do this outside of their own rigid academic context. I find the art-circuit context rather oppressive. I have some experience of it in the USA, where there is an attitude that artists who get too much into teaching are basically people who have failed as artists and are teachers who, being frustrated artists cannot be good teachers. This attitude is one of which we have to be very wary. Obviously, it is possible for artists to be artists and for teachers to be teachers, and one does not exclude the other. The interesting aspect of Great Britain is that even though for a very long time the economic climate has been bad - which we in Germany have experienced only in the past six months - the art world is lively because there are many colleges, which makes it possible for many artists somehow to survive. They don't have to drive taxis, they don't have to tend bars, and they are still working, intellectually, within their own sphere of interest. These colleges enable them to be artists at the same time. They also have an openness from rock'n'roll ideas. This is something we do not really have in art schools in Germany because they are more established, respectable institutions. In Germany it is surprising how many independent artists, some of them very successful, take pride in being appointed as professors, not only because it pays well but also because it is a matter of social prestige.

Regarding the different programmes in Germany, Düsseldorf, in particular, is rather well known because Beuys tried to revolutionise it, and also used it for his own strategy. It has become a very traditional kind of art academy in the way it represents itself, but nevertheless there are ten or twelve artists teaching there who are completely independent of this, who do their own thing. Quite a number of students come out of the schools, and their number in itself makes them independent and this creates a momentum. This is important because critical knowledge expands and superficial ways of dealing with art can be questioned by the talented people who have been to these schools, particularly those who are art teachers and whose expectations of getting jobs as artists are very slim.

The subject of opportunities that are created for students, or each individual student, is something that we suppress. We do not question the fact that we are producing what is considered by sociologists to be the academic proletariat. We state very clearly that there are no reasons at all why anyone should become an artist or go to art school. Just because you have been to art school doesn't mean that you are an artist and therefore society should support you because you think you are an artist. It has to be said, over and over again, that it would be immoral to encourage expectations that can't be fulfilled. The relationship to students is permanently one in which you build them up, where you support and encourage. At the same time I find it absolutely necessary to destroy illusions. Go to the library, I will say, look at this, this has been done much more thoroughly. One has to confront students with the stupidity of producing art that mindlessly sticks within certain conventions, without having some inner necessity to do so. This is very cruel, but these two elements do belong together, and thank God that we have such different characters, so many different backgrounds, so many different mentalities, so that students take on roles that keep the critical climate going. Often it is impossible to tell students they're no good, that they're not really working or to suggest that they should leave the school.

The question is: when do students leave school? More and more students try to extend their presence at school as a kind of artificial paradise, mostly for social reasons. They have free social insurance, medical insurance and so on. It is possible, in most of the academies in Germany, to become a Masters pupil, which means that for one year - two semesters - they have a studio space and that is a form of support that means they don't have to rent their own studio.

I believe that the most severe and cruel time for students is the two and a half years after leaving school because nobody knocks at their door, nobody tells them to get up. We have to prepare them for this extreme isolation and, ultimately, an old fashioned-kind of loneliness.

The problem of the "star" system, which was definitely a problem a couple of years ago, is fading now. Thank God for the recession in relation to the art world. Nevertheless it is a built-in problem, because students do have a tendency to over-idealise, which is a problem that needs to be overcome. However, this arouses very ambivalent feelings. Many students want to become a star. Sometimes they are very aggressively against the system just to make sure that they do not become a star, often because it would be unlikely for them to achieve this status anyway. This is where, I think, a therapeutic approach comes in; it is necessary to be open and deal with this head-on as a psychological problem. This problem exists in all professional spheres, but it exists in the arts in a completely overstated sense. Yet if this overstated sense did not exist there might not be a motive for doing such impossible things as art. I do not have the answer to that, but I'm very much aware of it.

At the moment we are confronted in our school with a couple of extremely complex people with difficult backgrounds. We have accepted a couple of students purely because we were so impressed by their courage in facing life; they were junkies or they were suicidal and saw creativity as the only possible way of rebuilding their existence. Generally they are an exception - we have not told them that the reason for accepting them was basically a social reason - and quite often such people go on to be incredibly disciplined and responsible, and a very important element in classes in the school.

The ultimate criterion for the school is: the better the students the better the school; and the more diversity amongst the teachers and artists, the better the students can be. We are fortunate in that more than a third of our artists are from other European cultures. We have Per Kirkeby from Denmark, for example; Enric Miralles, the architect from Barcelona; and a number of colleagues from Austria; Peter Weibel, Peter Kubelka and Hermann Nitsch. So the diversity is very strong.

Frankfurt itself is the most unlikely place for art: it's a tough, very unattractive financial capital. There is no such thing as an art world; there is no bohemian atmosphere. There was a strong left-wing political tradition but it doesn't exist any more. A relatively small town that was completely destroyed in the war, it is now like a Morris Minor with a Roll Royce engine. It's very high pitched and has a lot of energy. It's very diverse: two thirds of the population are foreigners. There seems to be no conflict at all, at least not in the working context, although if the economy goes further into recession we fear that tension will build up. Problems that we thought we had overcome - nationalism or religious fanaticism or xenophobia - all these things are creeping back. When we discuss these issues we always refer back to the fact that we are in an art school and that aesthetic articulation is ultimately very political. We say that we should not give ourselves social alibis but should have a social outlook, yet we should also be discriminating and critical towards art.

Obviously it is necessary to establish examples that we can check critically, so we have an exhibition space in which we invite artists to hold exhibitions; these stimulate ideas for assignments and seminars. Teaching guest professors have been recruited through this exhibition space. They have checked out the situation and found it interesting to come for a year, or even two or three years, to teach.

In Germany people are pensioned when they are 55. We are currently trying to invite two old artists, one 73 and one 85, into the school. They would not be paid very much because they have an income but we would give them a studio, just because we think that grandparents have a much easier and safer relationship with their grandchildren than parents have with their children. Obviously they are people with a lot of experience, who have a clear notion of why they would like to have a studio as working artists in the school. It is not just that they can drink their bottle of red wine, and chat; also that it's very important for them to become familiar with an understanding of the different meanings of art at a particular time - not just in an ideological sense but in a social, political and economic sense.

Now, the word "Academy" has been posed here, in the title **The Artist and the Academy**. We don't call ourselves an academy, even though we are one of the few art schools that actually is an academy. The word has been inflated so much that you can now have your fingernails polished and this is called the fingernail academy. So we insist on the old-fashioned term "school", but not without an argument about the bad, bad world of management culture (I'm referring here to the Harvard School of Business, even though I've not been there and don't know it). Another reason why Academy is not used very much by art schools in Germany is that The Academy, that is, the National Academy of the Arts, which was created by reuniting one academy from West Germany and one from East Germany is something that comes from the Emperor, from the Kaiser. It is very backward-looking, driven by a completely fascistic tendency. They are trying to put these broken pieces together again, which is a highly questionable activity. You have late capitalist art from the 1950s and Stalinist art from East Germany in this academy together.

Institutions that have gone through many changes, which have been threatened by success, and by different political directions, must have the potential to regenerate themselves and also to bide their time. The Americans have a wonderful saying that there is a time to bite and a time to chew. We have had a very active period that was generously sponsored by the City, now we are in a really tight spot because our budget has been cut. This is a really interesting challenge because it gives us an opportunity to get rid of three jobs in the administration that have slowly grown along with all the teachers, professors and other things. It seemed to be necessary for the administration to grow, not because of the work that had to be done but as a kind of unspoken agreement, that if you benefit the administration benefits, too. So the idea now is to cut down on some administration. I can't wholeheartedly approve, but we have to survive and I hope we can make the best of it.

We never think of the school as a professional school in the sense of making professional artists so we teach only in areas that are non-applied. But it is necessary that all the areas of the visual arts are included. It's just a question of achieving the right balance, and having the right people in the right place at the right time. We have to make sure that there are competitive people, younger people who have a different point of view and who are perhaps thinking in a completely different direction but nevertheless do identify with the place. I think the best schools of this kind are those that do not have too many similar ideas of the artist, that do not form a sort of programme that becomes orthodox. When we have a goal that we seem to agree on, and when there is a formal agreement in terms of style, that, I think, works against dialogue. We have Civil Service appointments, which come with tenure. This is not so much the practice in England, and it is an incredible privilege because we who have this tenured position can leave at any time yet the State can't throw us out unless we do something criminal. Even if we don't go to work it is very difficult to throw us out.

Ultimately, our daily work has to deal with risk. We don't have to have definite answers, but we have to be able to take risks and, when we have failed state clearly that we know we have failed, so we are learning on the job. It is an extremely exhausting situation because students can really gobble you up, they suck you dry. You have to make sure that you get something out of it on your side. What is so positive in England, which we unfortunately don't have, is many more assistant teaching posts. We have a much more static situation, with full-time professors, a few adjunct guest professors, and some postgraduate students who are like tutors or teaching assistants but only for a year, or three or four terms. What we don't have is a kind of momentum of critical intellectual younger people who are hungry for the job of the professors, and who would do it much better than laid-back professors.

It is basically a special structure that has to be kept open all the time, and has to be questioned. The educational discussion should never take place in a back room, in a kitchen-cabinet manner. It should be held in front of the students, with people espousing ideas on aesthetic grounds, not on personal grounds. I believe that is the best set-up possible, and when there is a social, aesthetic, political and economic dimension this becomes quite clear. We have insisted that all our salaries can be seen by anyone who wants to see them who is part of the school (we don't put them up on a blackboard). When we are working in public institutions we have to make clear that it is with public money, taxpayers' money; and that we feel this expenditure on us is completely justified. Even though many of us have questions about our effectiveness, we don't question the fact that we earn money, and that is as it should be. This contradiction exists, and one should be up-front about it. I think all this makes for a highly interesting education for students, because generally the students have an enlightened dilettantism, and sometimes the curiosity or scrutiny of some of the students and some of the teachers produces a highly critical debate.

I'm very sceptical about all these programmes of official exchanges between different art schools, these things should always happen very individually, I'm sceptical about all these European programmes of the

EU, because we could all end up not dealing with differences but dealing with sameness which have been devised by administrators who have no idea what is necessary for students, and have no idea what is necessary for artists or those who are involved in the schools. I have not given a paper in the usual sense, I felt it would be better to give you some idea of the school in Frankfurt, which is different from München, which is different from Berlin and hopefully different from other places. This is exactly what interests me - the difference much more than the sameness.

LIST OF CONTRIBUTORS

Nicholas de Ville   Head of Visual Arts, Goldsmiths' College, University of London

Stephen Foster   Director, John Hansard Gallery, University of Southampton

Thierry de Duve   Critic, and currently Lecturer, Massachusetts Institute of Technology

Colin Cina   Dean of Art, Chelsea College of Art and Design

Alexander Tzonis   Professor of Architecture, T.U. Delft

Liane Lefaivre   Critic, Author and Lecturer

Susan Hiller   Artist, and Associate Professor of Fine Art, University of Ulster

Iain Biggs   Head of Fine Art, University of the West of England

Kasper König   Rector, State Academy of Fine Art, Frankfurt